Behind the Walls

BEHIND
THE WALLS

*A Guide for Family and Friends
of Texas Inmates*

Jorge Antonio Renaud

Number One:
North Texas Crime and Criminal Justice Series

The University of North Texas Press
Denton, Texas

6 5 4 3 2 1

The paper in this book meets the minimum requirements of the American National Standard for Permanence of Paper for Printed Library Materials, Z39.48.1984

Permissions
University of North Texas Press
PO Box 311336
Denton, TX 76203-1336
940-565-2142

Library of Congress Cataloging-in-Publication Data

Renaud, Jorge Antonio, 1956–
    Behind the walls : a guide for families and friends of Texas prison inmates / Jorge Antonio Renaud.—1st ed.
        p.   cm. — (North Texas crime and criminal justice series ; no. 1.)
        Includes index.
        ISBN 1-57441-152-7 (cloth : alk. paper) — ISBN 1-57441-153-5 (pbk. : alk. paper)
        1. Prisons—Texas. 2. Prison administration—Texas. 3. Prisoners—Texas.
    I. Title. II. Title: Guide for families and friends of Texas prison inmates. III. Series.
    HV9475.T4R46 2002
    365'.6'09764—dc21

    2002009176

Behind the Walls: A Guide for Family and Friends of Texas Inmates is Number One:
North Texas Crime and Criminal Justice Series

Photographs by Alan Pogue
Design by Angela Schmitt

Dedication

Para mis tres mujeres;
mi ama, Marina, por su amor;
mi esposa, Lisa, por su fe;
y mi hija, Catarina, por su vida.

For my three women;
my mother, Marina, for her love;
my wife, Lisa, for her faith;
my daughter, Catarina, for her life.

Contents

Acknowledgments

Writing from prison, with few resources and in the face of institutional hostility, can be a frustrating, despairing, and enlightening experience. This book would not have been possible without the assistance of my brothers Esteban and Roberto, my sister Susana, and my father. Thanks to Scott Nowell for the unit profiles and legal nudges, and to Sheldon DeLuca and Rudy Rios for technical help. And thank you, Lisa, for never flinching at my tantrums and requests/demands.

Introduction

I am going to tell you about Texas prisons. Forget what you've seen in the movies. Forget what you've read in newspapers, and what you are shown for a few minutes on your local news. The media, which seldom can be rightfully accused of purposely misinforming Texans about their prisons, nevertheless relies on official sources for its news. Newspapers and news stations rarely show you an inmate's view of prison. What is important to the prison director may not be important to the inmate's wife, or mother, or son.

I first came to prison in 1977, left for eight months in 1979-80, returned in May of 1980, paroled in 1987, returned in 1991 and will not leave until at least 2006. Despite my criminal history, I am an intelligent, educated man, and for years I have considered how I might address the problems that face convicts and their families. Because, for decades, those who care about inmates have been kept in the dark when it comes to almost every imaginable facet of prison life. They have been forced to rely on officials—who often have treated them with the contempt those officials feel for inmates—or they have been forced to depend on the inmates themselves, many of whom are inarticulate, do not understand the system themselves and thus cannot explain it, or will simply not tell the truth, even to their families.

In turn, without meaningful help, many convicts have never addressed the personal problems that caused their criminal behavior. They then returned to prison, leaving behind shattered lives and children who, more often than not, followed in their criminal footsteps.

What I say may surprise you. It may bore you. It may horrify you. It will surely anger some Texas Department of Criminal Justice (TDCJ) officials, who would prefer you remain unaware of the differences between official policy and daily practice. What I say will anger certain inmate groups, who would prefer the public not know of their existence, much less their aims and methods. Within the limits of respect and reason, I don't care if I offend those two groups.

The friends and families of inmates are also victims, torn between their sympathies for the people directly affected by criminals and their empathy for their sons, daughters, fathers, brothers, sisters, mothers, and friends in prison. Their loyalty will not allow them to abandon their loved ones, even as they struggle with shame, embarrassment, disbelief and maybe disgust at what those loved ones did. Their plight is a difficult, long-ignored gray area in prison politics. I hope this book helps them.

I want to point out a few things you should keep in mind while you read the topics I will later discuss in depth.

1. Almost everything that concerns inmates—where and how often they are allowed to recreate; whether they are allowed contact visits; when they will become eligible for parole; everything is affected by their *custody level,* sometimes referred to as their *status*. I will refer to both frequently. They are the same. For all intents and purposes, any penal institution in Texas that is surrounded by razor wire and guarded by armed guards with orders to shoot escapees is a maximum-security facility. Custody levels are simply the classes within each institution that govern how much freedom and how many privileges inmates have within that particular prison. More about this in chapter one.

2. In any particular prison, the warden is *God.* I do not exaggerate. Some guards tremble when the warden comes around. He, or she, sets policy, hands out favors and decides by his or her actions the tone and mood of that unit. This is important to remember. If you are confronted with a policy contrary to those described in this book at a unit your son or daughter is assigned to, it is most probably because of a warden's direct order or indirect approval.

3. In every Texas prison, security is the most important thing on any guard's mind. Security is simply preventing escapes, and any action or person who helps or encourages an inmate to escape affects security. Everything else is secondary, including staff and inmates' rehabilitative needs—*everything.*

   Two examples:

a) In 1974, Fred Gomez Carrasco took eleven hostages at the Walls Unit in downtown Huntsville and attempted to use them as shields in an escape attempt. A gun battle ensued. Two hostages were killed, along with two inmates. No one escaped. On almost every Texas prison, on at least one gate, a sign coldly declares, "No hostages exit through this gate." This is not for the inmates' benefit, but so all officers and staff will understand—inmates will not be allowed to buy their freedom by taking hostages, not in Texas.

b) In 1996, on the French Robertson Unit near Abilene, a guard fired a "warning" shot at an inmate he claimed was fleeing from an outside work squad. The "warning" shot struck the inmate between the eyes, killing him. There was no outside investigation. The annual Officer of the Year competition for the Robertson Unit was declared over by the unit warden, who honored the guard who had killed the fleeing "escapee."

So, if a policy seems strange to you, or goes opposite to what common sense says would best serve an inmate's personal needs, ask yourself, "How does this policy enhance the security of this unit?"

4) I refer to all prison personnel as staff. TDCJ policy makes a distinction—officers wear gray and are considered law enforcement personnel, at least to a degree. Staff members —nurses, counselors, chaplains, maintenance, and industry supervisors— wear street clothes and are not involved in the day-to-day supervision of inmates. When I say staff in this book, however, I am speaking of any person employed by the state and involved in a prison's administration, unless I specifically note otherwise. The reason for this is that every person working within TDCJ walls has the power to write disciplinary reports on inmates, which affect the inmates' custody and thus their parole eligibility. So, it makes little difference to us what clothes they wear when they wield such power over us.

5) I will refer to inmates throughout this book as "he." This is not

an attempt to slight or ignore the female inmates. It is a recognition that, except for minor housekeeping and medical facets aside, females undergo the same tribulations, are affected by the same policies, must adhere to the same regulations and are treated the same by TDCJ staff. Where they truly differ—in their needs as pregnant women and as mothers—is an area I have addressed in the chapter on medical care.

A Short History of Texas Prisons

In order to understand the Texas prison system and how it deals with inmates and their families, you need to know a little of Texas prison history and the psychology that drives prison officials.

First, prisons don't make money for the state, and this irritates bureaucrats to no end—that, with more than 100,000 able-bodied, convicted criminals at their disposal, the Texas Department of Criminal Justice (TDCJ) cannot be labor intensive enough to at least break even, or make a dollar, as it used to. At one time, under the convict lease system—in which corporations or wealthy individuals would lease convicts from the state for private use—enough money was made so that Texas didn't need to appropriate funds from prisons. Convicts used to be leased to railroads, plantations, and mining corporations. However, the lessors—Ward Dewey Corporation of Galveston, which leased the entire penitentiary from 1871 to 1877; E. H. Cunningham and L. A. Ellis, who leased Huntsville prison from January 1878 to March 1893; and many others—spread the wealth around. They paid Texas officials for the right to have their hired prisoners pile up the profits.

By 1910, corruption in the prison system was so pervasive that the fountain of wealth—the leasing system—was abolished in a wave of reform, but scandals continued. During Miriam "Ma" Ferguson's reign as governor, she and her husband, ex-governor "Pa" Ferguson, were accused of pardoning an average of one hundred convicts monthly for payments in cash or land. Their excesses led to a state amendment that abolished the Board of Prison Committee and established a nine-member Texas Prison Board—which essentially just served the purpose of trading riders in mid-race.

The gravy train rolled on. (If early prison board members believed in rehabilitation, they did so in secrecy, except for perhaps Thomas J. Goree. As prison superintendent from 1878 to 1891, Goree believed that the Lord would lead one rightly, even if one was a Texas convict. Accordingly, he established weekly worship classes with rudimentary training in basic subjects, and he set up a library with a few thousand volumes.) During the 1930s, Texas governors avoided prison issues and continued to sell pardons at generous prices. A happy face was put on prison conditions, mostly through good public relations efforts. The Texas Prison Rodeo, a wild-West extravaganza featuring convict cowboys hurling their untrained bodies in front of wild bulls in exchange for applause and a few dollars, began its fifty-five-year run in Huntsville in 1931. An all-convict cast was featured on Fort Worth's "Thirty Minutes Behind the Walls," a radio program that put a positive spin on prison life.

But little was in fact positive. Reports of unsanitary living conditions, of atrocities committed by employees and of mysterious deaths of convicts persisted and were just as persistently ignored. The system instead threw money, as it always has, at improving security and increasing its industrialization. Oscar B. Ellis, who in 1948 was appointed to head the system, talked the Legislature out of funds and promptly increased expenditures for fences, floodlights, and picket towers. George Beto, who succeeded Ellis, expanded the industrial scope of the then-Texas Department of Corrections, developing a dental laboratory, garment factories, a bus-repair shop, a tire recapping facility, a coffee roasting plant, and other industries, all implemented to increase the cost effectiveness of what was supposedly the country's most peaceful, well-run prison system. It had to be the best run, most peaceful system, because, after all, unlike New York's Attica state prison and unlike the California system, the Texas Department of Corrections (TDC) did not erupt in violence in the 1960s. Texas convicts were all gainfully employed in meaningful trades; all were serving out their sentences brimming with health and repenting willingly while under the benevolent eyes of the fair but firm TDC.

But it was untrue, and by the early 1970s a determined band of prison writ-writers, assisted by a wisp of an Eastern interloper and a crusty East Texas judge, filed an extraordinary series of lawsuits that exposed the brutalities in TDC and forced massive, structural changes. These changes didn't come easy. Until 1964, United States courts had adopted a hands-off attitude toward prisons, showing total deference to administrators whenever prisoners complained about conditions. Inmates trying to get into the federal courts faced daunting procedural barriers, not to mention severe harassment from prison officials—harassment that in Texas often included beatings by both staff and their lackeys, the building tenders, or inmate guards.

In most instances, inmates were not allowed to assist each other in preparing writs. They were allowed limited, if any, access to lawbooks, and each Texas unit had its own rules regarding who could visit the law library—if one existed on that unit—and how legal materials could be stored. Prisoners' correspondence with attorneys was often destroyed. Inmates trying to have their writs notarized had to get the approval of prison officials, who served as notary public officials inside prison. As a result, those officials were then put on notice that they were the subjects of those same lawsuits, with predictable results—harassment of the inmates filing the writs. Inmates existed in a land where the Constitution was but a rumor, and its rights did not extend to them.

Cracks appeared in that wall when the U.S. Supreme Court, in 1964, ruled that Muslim prisoners asking access to the Quran and opportunities to practice their religion did indeed have the right to challenge the practices of prison officials. Five years later, the gap widened as the Supreme Court, ruling in *Johnson v. Avery*, frowned on Tennessee regulations prohibiting convicts from helping each other in legal matters. Writing for the majority, Justice Abe Fortas said, "[U]nless and until the state provides some reasonable alternative to assist inmates in the preparation of petitions for post-conviction relief, it may not validly enforce a regulation . . . barring inmates from furnishing such assistance to other prisoners." *Johnson v. Avery*, 89 S.Ct. 747 (1969).

Inmates, and the lower courts, took notice. Across the country, especially in the plantation-type Southern prisons, inmates began to file legal protests that increasingly found the ears of federal jurists. In 1970, a federal district court declared the entire Arkansas State Penitentiary unconstitutional and was upheld by a higher court. *Holt v. Sarvar*, 412 F.2d 304 (8th Cir. 1971). In 1974, the medical care provided by the Alabama prison system was declared constitutionally inadequate, a decision also upheld by a higher court a few years later. *Newman v. Alabama*, 559 F.2d 283 (5th Cir. 1977). The Mississippi Prison system was declared unconstitutional in 1975, a decision upheld by the 5th Circuit. *Gates v. Collier*, 501 F.2d 1206 (5th Cir. 1977).

Two factors enabled inmates to topple entrenched prison systems: activist judges taking their cue from the Supreme Court, and a novel approach that looked not at one aspect of a prison—which by itself might not violate constitutional standards—but at its entire operation.

In the Mississippi case of *Gates v. Collier*, the court commented that, "Each factor separately may not rise to constitutional dimensions; however, the effect of the totality of those circumstances is the infliction of punishment on inmates violative of the Eighth Amendment." Meanwhile, writ-writers in what was then the TDC had found an advocate whose assistance would be pivotal in the events to come. Frances Jalet, an Eastern lawyer who had felt the sting of gender discrimination, came to work for the Legal Aid and Defender Society of Travis County. She had begun to visit inmate Fred Cruz, then at the Ellis Unit, in 1967. With her urging and assistance, Cruz and Robert Novak filed a petition protesting the TDC rule prohibiting inmates from assisting one another in legal matters. Although their writ, *Novak v. Beto*, 453 F2d 661 (5th Cir. 1971), was denied by the Fifth Circuit, it was on the edge of a shift—away from the blanket approval of all claims made by prison administrators and toward the more exacting standard then being applied to other Southern prisons.

Texas inmates continued pounding at the gates. In October of 1971, the Fifth Circuit sent back to district courts a case claiming constitutional violations by prison regulations on an issue that had already been addressed by numerous federal courts—inmates helping other inmates with legal assistance. Reluctantly but firmly, the court concluded that, "[I]nterference with federally guaranteed rights may not be insulated on the basis that everything which occurs within prison walls is protected as prison administration." *Rocha v. Beto* 449 F2d, 741. Director Beto reacted predictably—he ordered TDC wardens to ban Frances Jalet from visiting her clients in prison, thus effectively severing communication between Jalet and her inmates. The uproar from Texas attorneys was immediate. Members of the state's more prestigious firms raised the roof and were backed by a concerned attorney general's office. Beto offered a compromise—he would transfer all of Jalet's prisoner clients to one prison and allow her to visit them there.

Of all the miscalculations and mistakes made by TDC officials during the *Ruiz v. Estelle* era, none was bigger than this. Beto's decision was predicated on his belief that, gathered under one prison and under the watchful eye of Warden Carl "Beartracks" McAdams—not known as a lover of inmates in general and of writ-writers in particular—the band of jailhouse lawyers would be intimidated and disband.

McAdams did what he could to expedite just that. He created a work squad for the group, the infamous Eight Hoe, which was forced to perform the most demanding jobs on the unit. None of the writ-writers were allowed to attend Windham school or college classes. They were denied many recreational and commissary privileges, on the flimsiest of reasons. But regardless of obstacles, the time they were now able to spend together enabled them to share information, tactics, and strategy. The isolation and harassment they faced fused them into a band with one purpose—to use the courts to change the system that was trying to crucify them.

Within one year, the group filed four class-action suits that were instrumental in shaping Texas prisons over the next three decades: (1) *Guajardo v. Estelle*, 580 F.2d 748 (5th Cir. 1978), which transformed TDC correspondence rules, (2) *Lamar v. Coffield*, 353 F. Supp. 1081, which ultimately desegregated the system, (3) *Corpus v. Estelle*, 551 F.2d 68 (5th Cir. 1977), which forced TDC to finally remove all restrictions against "jailhouse lawyering"; and, of course, (4) *Ruiz v. Estelle*, 503 F. Supp. 1265 (5th Cir. 1980).

In prison lore, Judge William Wayne Justice picked the petition of David Ruiz—handwritten on toilet paper—off a stack of similar complaints. The judge himself said that Ruiz's writ was chosen from among the others because Ruiz—an Austin native, who had been in and out of prison since his teens—had complained about a range of issues, and that best fit the "totality of circumstances" standard then being adopted by higher courts. Justice was not immune to his role in the case and to the criticism that he took too active a role in it, but he was inured to it. While on the bench of the Eastern District, he had ordered the integration of East Texas schools and a restructuring of the Texas Youth Council—the state's reform schools—and was widely reviled by many of the state's more conservative citizens for his willingness to become involved.

In a 1990 speech at a Stanford University, Justice explained his actions and made a compelling argument that activism is at times called for to keep the Constitution viable. He recalled that, early in his career as a sitting judge, he was struck by the inept attempts by prisoners to present grievances against the state and by the obviously unfair advantage prison officials had. "I was more than troubled by this state of affairs; I was offended by it," Justice said. "Given the fact that TDC was always represented by counsel, while prisoners had to appear *pro se*, and given the consequences that inevitably followed, one side of a controversy was routinely going unheard. This, it seemed, and it still seems, did not accord with the goals and aspirations of our adversarial system of justice," the judge said. In other words, Justice believed it was his duty to allow the prisoners the chance to present their complaints and to provide them with an attorney who could navigate the legal maze the state's attorneys were sure to erect. In doing this, Justice admits his role in kick-starting events but defends them as a search for the truth.

"I have no hesitation in accepting that what I did can properly be called judicial activism," Justice said. "I was surely not passive. No one told me to consolidate those cases. No one told me to file a motion for an attorney. I simply wanted to know what was going on." And he found out, as did the state's citizens, in 159 days of testimony by hundreds of witnesses—inmates, guards, and attorneys. Ruiz and the other petitions that Justice had consolidated into one case accused W. J. Estelle, who had succeeded Beto as prison director, of: (1) running a corrupt empire that granted select inmates life and death control over other convicts, (2) ignoring the medical and psychological needs of Texas convicts and allowing other inmates to become pseudo-doctors who were allowing to diagnose and treat illnesses without the slightest training, (3) warehousing three and four inmates in cells designed for one, (4) arbitrarily tossing inmates into dungeon-like solitary confinement without the slightest nod to due process, (5) denying and indeed actively preventing inmates from pursuing relief in the courts.

Estelle and the state's lawyers denied it all. But on December 12, 1980, in a ringing denunciation to the state, Justice issued an opinion finding for Ruiz and his fellow inmates in words that bear repeating:

> "The trial of this action lasted longer than any prison case—and perhaps any civil rights case—in the history of American jurisprudence. In marked contrast to prison cases in other states, the

defendant prison officials here refused to concede that any aspect of their operations were unconstitutional, and vigorously contested the allegations of the inmate class on every issue . . . It is impossible for a written opinion to convey the pernicious conditions and the pain and degradation which ordinary inmates suffer within the TDC walls—the gruesome experience of youthful first offenders forcibly raped; the cruel and justifiable fears of inmates, wondering when they will be called upon to defend the next violent assault; the sheer misery, the discomfort, the wholesale loss of privacy for prisoners housed with one, two, or three others in a forty-five foot cell or suffocatingly packed together in a crowded dormitory; the physical suffering and wretched psychological stress which must be endured by those sick or injured who cannot obtain adequate medical care; the sense of abject helplessness felt by inmates arbitrarily sent to solitary confinement or administrative segregation without proper opportunity to defend themselves or to argue their causes; the bitter frustration of inmates prevented from petitioning the courts and other governmental authorities for relief from perceived injustices . . . But those iniquitous and distressing circumstances are prohibited by the great constitutional principles that no human being, regardless of how disfavored by society, shall be subjected to cruel and unusual punishment or be deprived of the due process of the law within the United States or America . . ." *Ruiz v. Estelle*, at 1391.

The impact of *Ruiz v. Estelle* is incalculable. The state finally did away with the hated building tenders, and as a result had to embark on a massive hiring spree to bring the ratio of guards to prisoners to an agreed-upon six-to-one. To comply with the population caps ordered by Justice—and to institute the mandated changes in cell and dormitory space – the state was forced to upgrade old prisons and build new ones, a costly and time-consuming procedure that was begun while the state, under the pressure of population caps, was forced to release thousands of convicts with only minimal review and safeguards. The result was foreseeable. A few convicts committed heinous acts that raised a tremendous outcry from Texans as to why the TDC was releasing so many prisoners. Among them, Kenneth Allen McDuff, whose sentence for the 1966 murders of three teenagers was commuted to life in prison, and who was released in 1989. In 1993 he killed again and was executed in 1998. He was also suspected in the murders of more than a dozen other women. The changes resulting from the public response are collectively called the "McDuff Rules."

Legislators, sensing the mood, screamed for reforms in the parole process, which necessitated more prison space. Texans approved billions of dollars for more prisons, which were, in the recession-laden 1980s, seen as economic boons to depressed, mostly rural communities. As a result of all those forces, a prison-building boom resulted in a newly named TDCJ, which is comprised of approximately 140 units, houses 140,000 prisoners, employs 25,000 guards and is by far the largest, most costliest state agency. But, without a doubt, the system has improved. Throughout this book, I'll refer to pre-*Ruiz* policy or pre-*Ruiz* conditions as a way of signifying or amplifying the differences wrought by that case.

In June of 2002, Judge William Wayne Justice signed a two-sentence order effectively removing TDCJ from federal oversight. It remains to be seen if state prison officials adhere to the reforms mandated by twenty-two years of court supervision.

CHAPTER ONE

diagnostic

Since October 1, 1849, when a horse thief became the first person to be held in the state's custody instead of by local law enforcement, Huntsville has been synonymous with Texas prisons. The beautiful town of Huntsville—nestled in the midst of the state's most lovely forests; four votes from being state capital instead of Austin; adopted home of General Sam Houston—is, nonetheless, by virtue of that first prison, fated to always be linked with prisons in the minds of Texans. That unit, built in what would soon be downtown Huntsville and known as the Walls, also soon included the growing system's administrative offices. Over a century later, as the system began to expand rapidly, it became obvious that a separate unit was needed as a processing center. The Diagnostic Unit, built in 1964 a few thousand yards from the original Walls, became that intake unit. While there are now other units that may also serve some of the functions as the Diagnostic Unit, (now called the Byrd Unit), it was the first, it remains the most thorough, and it is the one I will use as a model.

Once men and women are sentenced to prison, they wait in the county jail until they "catch the chain" to Huntsville. That phrase—probably a reference to either the way inmates were chained together outside overflowing small jails or to one-time chain-gang work squads—means to be transported, by county or state vehicle, to prison. TDCJ does not allow inmates to keep their clothes, radios, televisions, books, etc., but neither does it give inmates advance warning that they will be on a particular chain on a given day. If you have been convicted and are awaiting transportation to Huntsville, it is best that you have someone pick up all that you can not take with you. The only items allowed to each inmate are a watch, a wedding ring, a chain and religious medallion, and a pair of shoes. If inmates have cash money, it will be taken and deposited into an account in the inmate's name and number after arrival. Incoming inmates should understand that if their jewelry and shoes are gaudy and/or expensive, other inmates will try to steal them. Since TDCJ sells inexpensive watches and shoes, I advise inmates to bring only an inexpensive chain with attached religious medallion, and, if married, a small wedding band. Anything else will attract attention and trouble. The first few hours at Diagnostic are by turns boring—inmates sit around in shorts and socks for hours at a time—and terrifying, at least to new inmates. The officers do what they can to impress inmates with the seriousness of the situation, and their gruff demeanor and harsh commands usually intimidate the newer inmates. Most experienced convicts are used to this, but "drive-ups" are noticeable by their bug-eyed faces and rigid postures. While stories of violent "testing" of new inmates by other inmates are mostly true, this will happen, if at all, upon arrival at one's assigned unit, not at the Diagnostic Unit.

TDCJ does not allow long hair or facial hair on male inmates; so all males get a burr, are ordered to shave, and may have to submit to a spraying of intimate areas with disinfectant. Inmates are allowed to spend a few dollars on necessary items and are assigned to cells. Although TDCJ has a policy of integrating inmates regardless of their prejudices, this will not happen until inmates arrive at their assigned units. While on Diagnostic, all inmates are assigned cellmates of the same race and roughly similar age and criminal history. This is to avoid violence before the system gets a chance to identify those prone to violence.

The purpose of Diagnostic is to examine inmates in order to better classify them so they will present the least security risk to TDCJ. Any talk about an inmate's rehabilitation and personal needs is way down the list of priorities. This is important: the system is not there to rehabilitate, to perform surgery, or to provide education or substance abuse counseling. Those may be a by-product of prison, but they take a back seat to security. The mission of TDCJ is to incarcerate convicted criminals and to ensure they don't escape. Becoming aware of physical and mental problems that may threaten the efficient running of a prison is part of incarceration. That is why Diagnostic exists—to physically, mentally, emotionally, and psychologically test inmates and assign them to units where they will present the least amount of security risk.

For example: if an inmate's knee problem is not discovered and he later claims it was created or worsened through TDCJ negligence, the funds and manpower wasted disproving that assertion detract from the incarceration mission of the system. Fixing the knee is a by-product of that concern. If an inmate has psychological problems that should be addressed and corrected before that inmate can safely return to society and contribute to society is of little concern to TDCJ. Identifying those problems is only important in case they might contribute to a violent attack on staff or inmates or perhaps lead that inmate to attempt to escape. All testing is geared to dig out anything that may cause problems for TDCJ. Any benefit the inmates receive is coincidental.

Inmates are given hearing, eye, and dental examinations, which are as thorough as can be expected, given the cattle-call aspect of the health care provided through the managed health care system. Inmates are given IQ tests and something called an Educational Achievement (EA) test, which the system uses to have some sort of standard for admittance into the vocational courses offered in prison but that has little free-world relevance. Inmates are interviewed by sociologists and quizzed about their criminal, social, institutional, educational, employment, family, military, and substance abuse history. If it is determined that an inmate has lied in his responses, he may be given a disciplinary case. TDCJ takes the diagnostic process seriously, because that is how inmates are classified, and classification leads to custody levels, which *affect security*.

There are four levels of custody—minimum, medium, close, and maximum, or administrative segregation (ad seg). (See chapter six for a more detailed explanation of administrative segregation and protective custody.) Initial custody assignments are determined by an inmate's length of sentence, age, charge, and by his behavior in the county jail and in Diagnostic itself. As I said in the introduction, almost every Texas prison is maximum security. Custody applies to the directness of supervision and degree of freedom that inmates have within a particular unit. Minimum custody inmates have more freedom and privileges than medium custody inmates, who have more freedom and privileges than close custody inmates, who for the most part have more freedom and privileges than inmates in ad/seg. (I'll clear up the "most part" in chapter six.)

However, and this may seem strange to those not familiar with prison: a convicted murderer sentenced to life can be in minimum custody, and a hot-check writer with a three-year sentence may be in close custody. Both may be in a maximum security environment, but a murderer who follows rules, keeps quiet, performs his assigned duties while showing no inclination to threaten the security of the unit (to escape), and does not threaten the staff or other inmates will be granted minimum custody status. The murderer may never be given a job outside the fence, but he will be allowed as much freedom within the fence and will be awarded as many privileges as a non-violent, short-term offender. TDCJ, to a large extent, does not care what you did to get in prison—what matters is what you do within its fences.

The Reception and Diagnostic Center Classification Committee (RDCCC), now armed with the results of the tests and whatever personal evaluations were done by the sociologists and psychologists, will assign each inmate to a unit and recommend a custody level, good time-earning category, and may recommend a job assignment. Once an inmate arrives at his unit, he will be given a job and housing in line with his custody designation. The system tries, within limits, to assign inmates with similar characteristics together. It reserves certain units for certain types of offenders. Some are for first-time, youthful offenders, others for older convicts; some have special arrangements for the handicapped, some for the psychologically disturbed. But with more than 140,000 inmates, the best that can be done is to try for a balance—a racial balance, an age-group balance, and a balance between lifers and short-timers. There are exceptions.

If an inmate is twenty-two, in prison for the first time, has a five-year sentence for drug possession, no criminal history, and a degree in business administration, he may be classified a minimal risk and assigned to one of the smaller, medium-security units, or even be assigned to an outside trusty camp. Then again, he may go to the Robertson Unit and be assigned by the Unit Classification Committee to the field squads, where he immediately gets into fights because of his youthful appearance or his precise, educated diction. He will then be demoted in status, to medium or perhaps close custody, and have to do his sentence day for day.

It's a roll of the dice. While TDCJ strives for a mix, if an inmate fills a need, he will be assigned wherever and however that need is best met. Once in the system, at his assigned unit, he may find a way—via educational or vocational programs, mostly—to get transferred to a unit more conducive to his needs, but TDCJ doesn't consider those needs a priority, unless they are medical. *Do not* expect proximity to family to be a factor when inmates are assigned to their unit.

CHAPTER TWO

living quarters

*I*n prison, privacy is precious. Inmates need some place to brood, to read and write letters, to kneel and pray. There is no place to be by oneself, except for rare instances. What little privacy inmates have is in their living quarters.

Depending on the age of a particular unit and on an inmate's custody level, he will live in one of three fashions: single-celled, in administrative segregation; double-celled, in all close, most medium, and some minimum assignments; or in a dormitory, which is only for minimum-security inmates. While many inmates would prefer cells, ironically only close-custody inmates—who have few privileges to speak of—are guaranteed cells.

At the time *Ruiz v. Estelle* was heard, TDCJ consisted of eighteen units—sixteen for males and two for females. Their design was primarily the same—one long corridor, intersected at intervals by housing blocks that extended, wing-like, to both sides. Imagine a cross with eight arms instead of two and you have the idea. Each block contained from two to four tiers, with twenty-one to thirty-one cells per tier. Designed for one inmate, there were never less than two inmates assigned to each cell, and severe overcrowding—a main issue in *Ruiz*—resulted in three or sometimes four inmates living in a forty-five-foot space.

This particular design, coupled with a severe shortage of officers, was a nightmare for both inmates and staff. The pickets, which contained cell-door control and communications equipment, were in the hallway, at the head of the blocks. The officers, expected to control traffic in and out of the blocks and also watch the dayrooms, spent most of their shift in and around the picket. This meant that the tiers were rarely patrolled, and nothing could be seen from the pickets. No one knew what went on in the far reaches of the run and in the cells themselves, and much went on—rapes, beatings, killings, drug trafficking and consumption, etc.

If anyone you know lives on Eastham, Ellis, Estelle, Ferguson, Coffield, Beto I, Wynne, Diagnostic, Retrieve, Ramsey I, Goree, Darrington, Clemens, or Central, he may still live in one of those old cells. Construction may have added other wings with larger cells, but there is no way to enlarge those particular cells. Most are nine feet long, five feet wide and eight feet high. The overall space varies—from forty-five square feet to sixty square feet. Most have forty-five. The cells have two bunks, one over the other, attached to one wall, with maybe a thirty-inch aisle between the bunks and the other wall. There is a toilet—without either seat or lid—in one corner of the cell farthest from the door and a small sink in the other corner. There is no hot water. In fact, none of the cells in TDCJ have hot running water, except perhaps on the privately run pre-release units.

The storage area consists of two shelves directly over the bunk. On some units, lockers have been installed in place of the shelves so that property can be locked away. These lockers very in size, but average twenty-four inches wide, twelve inches tall, and eighteen inches deep. There is no desk, no stool, and no place to set any electrical appliances—fans, radios, typewriters—all must be placed on the floor or bed. A bare bulb lights the cells. The cells have no windows, as they are built into the buildings, away from the outer wall. The cells have poor circulation, are not air-conditioned, and are stifling in the summer and cold in the winter.

The newer units, reflecting the concerns raised in *Ruiz*, do not have many of these design problems and have many more amenities. The buildings that house inmates are of a pod-like design—the picket is in the center of the pod, with the cells built around it, and all cell doors face the picket. This allows the picket officer to visually monitor all cells, and the rover, or the officer on the floor, to stay in sight of the picket officer while he walks the blocks. The picket officer, with all door controls at his fingertips, can open one door or all of them as he sees fit, and can open and close one or all pod doors, thus effectively sealing off one block in case of trouble. Each pod usually consists of twenty-four two-man cells, on two or three tiers. The cells are much larger—eighty square feet. Each includes a twenty-four by thirty-six inch desk with attached stool, two shelves for electrical appliances and cosmetics, and two lockable storage units—each twelve by twenty-four by twenty-four inches.

The bunks are still stacked, but each has a window over it, which can be opened and closed by inmates. The cells are bright, with fluorescent lighting. While not air-conditioned, (except for ad/seg,) the cells have vents that ensure a flow of fresh air, and they are extremely well heated. Each cell has a polished steel mirror; wall hooks for clothes; steps built into the wall for the inmate who must climb off and onto the top bunk—all items the old cells don't include—basic as they seem. However, there is still one crucial item lacking—a way of notifying the officers in case of trouble in a locked cell.

Concerning security, the new design is only as efficient as the staff on duty. Few officers walk the runs, unless it is necessary to close the doors, or while taking count of the inmates. Few picket officers watch the cells—they instead read or talk with other officers via telephone or intercom. Inmates trapped with a violent cell partner, or inmates undergoing a medical emergency, are at the mercy of inattentive officers.

Another change provided by the new housing units is that each wing has four or five one-man showers, allowing inmates to shower at any time during the day. The old units have huge communal showers, with as many as a hundred inmates showering at once, at the time decided by the staff. The inmates on newer units may shower when they want, with a measure of privacy.

Dormitory life, while different from cell life, has not changed much throughout the years, except that inmates have more room and a bit more privacy. Before *Ruiz*, on some units, inmates were so cramped that you could have a bunk over you, one directly at your feet, one at your head, and one on either your left or right side, in what was basically one huge bunk. I quote here a relevant passage from *Ruiz*:

"The population density of inmates confined in dormitories is shocking. At the Central Unit, for example, two rows of double-decker bunks, adjacent to each other, run down the middle of the dormitory. The scene was described as resembling one giant bed. Except for his bed, an inmate in this dormitory has no assigned space. Even while asleep, an inmate so confined is within easy and immediate reach of three other inmates (those sleeping at his side, at his head, and at his feet), and he is directly above or below a fourth inmate. . . . Under both of these arrangements a total deprivation of privacy in insured, since every inmate is in full view of dozens of others at all times. Not even the urinals or toilets are screened or partitioned from the rest of the space." *Ruiz v. Estelle*, 503 F.Supp. at 1278.

The cramped conditions meant that inmates had no way to get away from each other—they were always within touching and smelling distance of each other. Given the shortage of staff, this meant there were innumerable fights over petty and not-so-petty arguments. Everyone knew what everyone else had, and theft was common. Life in the dormitories was a dreaded environment. Now each inmate in a dormitory lives in a cubicle, with four-foot high partitions enclosing each living space. (Exceptions are in transfer facilities, where some dorms still have bunks stacked on one another. TDCJ exempts these facilities from its new policy, stating they are temporary living quarters and thus don't fall under *Ruiz* stipulations.) Inmates in dorms have storage lockers under their bunks, away from curious eyes. Each cubicle encloses a small desk and a tiny shelf. The living area itself is approximately four by twelve feet.

One facet of dorm life that remains the same is the toilet facilities. A dorm may have from four to eight urinals and the same amount of toilets, situated at the same end of the dorm, all next to one another, and none are enclosed or partitioned in any way, except from actual sleeping areas. Any inmate using them has no privacy whatsoever. Some dorms have the toilet area within nineteen feet of the closest bunks. If on a newer unit, showers are one-man stalls. If not, inmates assigned to dorms must shower in the communal showers.

Any attempts to personalize living quarters are subject to restrictions decided upon by either the warden or the building major. Texas prisons are not like the ones you see in the movies—which are usually California state prisons, close to Hollywood—or federal prisons. We don't have televisions in our cells, except on the Walls and Ramsey I. We don't have posters on the wall. We aren't allowed to decorate. Some units will allow inmates to make picture frames of matches or toothpicks and to have pictures on their desks. Recognizing that many inmates wash their own clothes, some units allow temporary clotheslines to be strung from bunk to sink. But on most units, none of these things are allowed. The cells must be totally bare except for a Bible and a few cosmetic items on the desk, if there is a desk. Officers on those units are encouraged to go into cells and rip down any photos; to throw away any picture frames; to write disciplinary cases on any inmates who in any way try to personalize their cells or cubicles. On those units, the tension between guards and inmates is frightening.

This attitude, which is hard to justify since photos or clotheslines present no security risk, deepens the frustration that inmates feel, and it contributes to violence, both among inmates and toward staff. Some wardens understand this, especially the more veteran wardens, and they allow small personal touches in the convicts' living areas. Those wardens extend a measure of respect to convicts in return for a general compliance of more security-oriented regulations.

CHAPTER THREE

food

*I*nmates in Texas prison eat in the chow halls because they have to, not because they want. Any chef will tell you that the quality of a meal drops with the amount of people you have to feed. In TDCJ, minimally trained cooks prepare from 1,000 to 3,000 meals three times a day, under minimal quality standards, and with only the pride they and an occasional professional wearing TDCJ gray bring to their jobs. The courts have ruled, and rightly so, that good taste cannot be dictated. The standard applied to institutional meals is that they be hot and nutritious. In turn, state dieticians and various medical experts set out the nutritional standards TDCJ follows. Inmates get three meals a day, and if an inmate eats all that he is offered, he will be assured of the minimal daily requirements of vitamins and minerals that medical experts say he needs to survive.

Meals consist of: three four-ounce servings of three different vegetables; a four-ounce serving of beans; a scoop of potatoes or rice; a piece of meat (except at breakfast); two pieces of bread, or two biscuits, or a three inch square of cornbread; and dessert at lunch (which can be cake, pie, gelatin, or pudding). That's it. If you complain, or ask for more, chances are good that the staff will take your tray and order you from the chow hall.

Substitutions are left to the menu—rice instead of potatoes, two cookies instead of cake. But the basics will not change—so many ounces of vegetables, so many starches, beans, meat, and a dessert. There are units where inmates are allowed to serve themselves more vegetables and may take a larger portion of the main dish, if it is spaghetti or a casserole. Many units have placed a metal screen between the food and the inmates, who hand empty trays through a slot in the beginning of the serving line and are handed a full tray through another slot at the end of the line. But if there is no screen between those eating and those serving on a unit where the kitchen staff enforces the suggested servings, an inmate who asks for more food is likely to receive a disciplinary case for attempting to get another scoop of beans.

If this isn't enough to drive inmates crazy, they are also aware of the tremendous amount of food that the average chow hall throws away after each meal. But TDCJ chow hall officers are governed by the fear that if one inmate asks for and receives extra food, all will. Then the last inmates will have nothing to eat, thus grinding the huge machine to a halt, bringing sergeants and captains and majors into the chow hall looking for someone to blame. To the institutional mind, it's better to make extra food, give inmates the minimum and throw the surplus away.

On to the food itself. Contrary to popular belief, steak is never served in TDCJ. Meat portions will be: 1) pork, in its infinite varieties—chops, ham cutlets, fatty ribs (once or twice a year), pressed ham, and the ever-present "links" (steamed, baked or barbecued); 2) chicken, in either leg/thigh quarters or patties; 3) bologna or salami; 4) fish, of the breaded, processed type, supplemented by the occasional salmon patty or tuna salad; and 5) beef or rather a rubbery substance that the state swears is beef with added filler.

Fresh fruit is non-existent, except on Christmas and Thanksgiving, when inmates are given an apple and orange. (The Christmas and Thanksgiving meals are excellent, with most inmates given two trays of twice-a-year goodies.) The only fruit given inmates on a regular basis is dates, raisins, and prunes. Once or twice a week, with the breakfast meal, inmates receive a two-ounce serving of canned fruit, usually apples or applesauce. Watermelons and cantaloupes will be served for a week or two, when they are in season and there is enough after the Officers'

Dining Room [ODR] gets its allotment. There are no strawberries, grapes, or bananas.

Fresh vegetables are given when they are in season, and are usually limited to lettuce, tomatoes, carrots, beets, and many types of beans and greens. Inmates will never see fresh celery, asparagus, or cauliflower—nothing other than what is grown in TDCJ fields and picked by TDCJ inmates, and only what is not consumed by the ODR.

Inmates are served tea, punch, or water with their meals, and for breakfast are given a half-pint of milk and coffee. Most units try to have ice in the lunch and supper beverages, but that ice will be in the containers, not served with the drink itself, and I've gone months without drinking any beverage that was not room temperature. There is no way for inmates to get ice to their living quarters, but sometimes enterprising kitchen workers will smuggle bags of ice to their areas and sell them.

If an inmate can prove to the medical department that he, for one reason or another, has specific dietary needs—a low-sodium, high-caloric, or a diabetic diet—he will be issued a diet card and be fed accordingly, but it will be up to him to adhere to his diet. There is also a procedure for inmates who, through religious convictions, refuse to eat pork or any meat at all. If those inmates have expressed their religious objections via the chapel, they will be allowed to substitute cheese, non-pork bologna, or extra beans when pork is on the menu.

Inmates at all custody levels eat the same food. In fact, TDCJ issues a master menu to the entire system, since TDCJ issues the food to the different units from a central warehouse. So, except for small changes or for a particular vegetable grown on a unit due to a farm manager with a green thumb, if Ellis serves pork chops and mashed potatoes on Wednesday, so should Wynne and Coffield.

There are three exceptions to this. First, inmates on Level III of ad/seg are not fed dessert of any kind. Second, inmates who throw food at staff are given food loaf—a cake-like concoction of vegetables, oatmeal, meat, and maybe cornbread, blended together and cooked into slabs. Food loaf, which supposedly meets all of an inmate's nutritional needs, can nonetheless only be fed to an inmate for a week without breaking the routine with a hot meal. Third, inmates who are given Johnnies while they are on lockdown status. (See Chapter 18 for a detailed look at lockdowns.) A Johnny is a sack lunch, usually consisting of one meat or cheese sandwich, one peanut butter and jelly sandwich, and a piece of cake or some raisins. That's it. Chase it with water, if you want. Inmates on prolonged lockdowns lose lots of weight.

Inmates eat in cafeterias, are served on plastic trays and eat with plastic ware—no knives or forks, just an oval plastic utensil with three sharp prongs on the front edge, which we call a "spork." Beverages are served in plastic pitchers. Tray and pitchers were aluminum until not so long ago, but the "thooonnngg" of metal banging on inmates' heads made that a hazard in the violence-plagued 1980s.

Like all else in TDCJ, the food on a unit will reflect the attitude of the warden. I've seen wardens walk into a chow hall and eat with inmates, a sure way of ensuring that the food is as hot and tasty as a kitchen captain can make it, given enough inmates and spices. And I've seen wardens who cared only for the food in the ODR; or wardens who would throw their plate of food at the inmate serving it if they didn't like the shape of a biscuit and order all inmate ODR waiters reassigned to the Line; or wardens who kept so much pressure on kitchen personnel over trivialities that it was almost impossible to prepare quality food.

One particularly nasty habit of some staff is to deny inmates their meals on one pretext or another. The TDCJ rulebooks say inmates will be "afforded the opportunity" to eat three meals a day. This ambiguous wording is interpreted by many guards, with the approval of like-minded ranking officers, to mean that anything inmates do on their way to eat—talk in the hallway, step out of line—can be interpreted as the inmate *refusing* the opportunity to eat by his actions. Of course, a liberal application of this rule means that any officer can, at any time, deny inmates meal after meal, day after day, in effect starving inmates they wish to harass. I have seen guards pick on specific inmates, accuse them of committing small disciplinary infractions (which, if true, should be handled by writing the inmates a disciplinary case instead of denying them a meal) and order them back to their cells without eating. I have protested this practice many times, only to have officers deny they are doing anything wrong, or to say they have the right to do so and will continue to do so while ranking officers on the shift or units allow it.

If inmates have money, they will often spend most of it on food and supplement their meals with homemade dishes called "spreads." Cans of beans, chili, roast beef, enchiladas, or processed meat will be heated in hot pots, the contents mixed with corn chips, jalapenos, and maybe pickles, and then slapped between bread or spooned from a bowl. Some spreads look nasty, but after a day in the fields, when the meal in the chow hall is ham casserole—well, it tastes good and it fills you up.

Inmates do not have access to microwaves, or refrigerators, or Bunsen burners, or hot plates of any kind. Inmates who do not have money to buy food can usually scrounge up a few stamps, so there is always a market for food stolen from the kitchen. Hustling kitchen workers make sandwiches, hamburgers, or just meat packets, hire smugglers and send them to different living quarters, knowing there will be someone willing to pay a few stamps for a snack. Desirable items are cheese, peanut butter, bread, crackers, and anything that can be used to spice up packaged noodle soup—the staple of store-bought meals.

Inmates eat when they are told, usually when their living quarters are called. Breakfast is from 3:30 A.M. until about 5 A.M. Lunch starts around 9:30 A.M. and goes until 12:30 or so. Supper is usually from 3:45 P.M. until 6 P.M. Of all meals, the most frustrating is breakfast, at least from the view of inmates who must get up at 2:30 A.M, wait in the dayroom for thirty minutes, and are then fed one cold egg, one half-pint of milk, two cold biscuits, and some congealed, unsweetened, unbuttered oatmeal. Some units have the grill cooks on duty while breakfast is being served and thus serve eggs or pancakes hot. But most units cook their food hours prior to serving it and keep it on steam tables. As a result, the eggs, pancakes, and biscuits are rubbery, often cold, and practically inedible.

On many of the newer units, the chow halls are in different buildings from the living quarters. To get from one to another, inmates walk through covered hallways that are nonetheless open to the weather. They walk through snow and rain, and the doors to the cafeterias themselves are left open, either through guard caprice or due to some vague security concern. I have sat and eaten while snow was falling down my collar.

As I said at the beginning of this chapter—inmates eat in chow halls out of necessity, not for enjoyment.

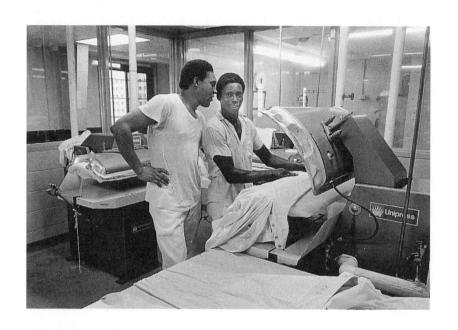

CHAPTER FOUR

clothing

*T*hink about what your taste in clothes says about you. Your wardrobe reflects your personality. Your grasp of fashion, your sense of color and texture, your hairstyle—all say something about your individuality.

The state prison does not want inmates to be individuals. It pursues policies that result in depersonalization, in a loss of personal identity, and it then justifies these policies in the name of security. There are various reasons for this. The first is that inmates who *look* like inmates - dressed similarly, and all unlike the general population – are easy to recognize if they escape. An inmate who walked out the front gate wearing jeans, a designer shirt, and a pair of brand-name tennis shoes would easily merge with everyone else. Depersonalization is also for the guards' benefit. If they do not see us as people, but as a mass of interchangeable inmates, they will not readily form associations with us. They will not have sympathy for us, show us leniency, or worse, bring us drugs and guns. Lastly, inmates who lose their sense of self are less likely to rebel. Texas inmates feel invisible. They feel that nothing they do is recognized. It is but one step from that to agreeing, subconsciously but sincerely, that if the others who dress like them, look like them, and act like them, are guilty and worthy of punishment, so are they.

The quickest way to depersonalize people is to have them all look the same. Texas inmates all look alike, except for physical features. Their clothes are interchangeable. They are not allowed color or style. They are not allowed any clothes from the free-world except for the shoes they wore to prison.

All Texas inmates wear white, short-sleeved, pullover shirts and white, slip-on pants. In recent years, TDCJ has done away with belts and buttons. Pants are of a pajama-like, expandable-waist type, without front openings. They are universally derided and detested. On a few units, some inmates with laundry connections have the old button-fly pants with front pockets made especially for them. They wash their own clothes and thus keep their "pocket pants," as they are called. But the new pants are what are issued and what the vast majority of inmates wear. They have only one pocket, in the left rear. Shirts also come with one small pocket, over the left breast.

State-issued shoes are either black low quarters or half boots. Inmates working outside are given a white, baseball-type cap. In cold weather, some inmates are issued long underwear. Every inmate is issued a green jacket during cold months and must turn it in during the spring so it can be clean and repaired for reuse. That's it—white shirts, pants, hats, and underwear, gray socks, green jackets. All of it interchangeable, none of it mine, except for a few instances.

The clothes we wear are ours only if we buy them in the commissary. (More on that in a minute.) We are issued our clothes when we turn in a dirty set. In addition to our clothes, we are issued a towel and a motel-sized bar of soap daily, and two sheets and a pillowcase weekly. It's exchanged on a one-for-one basis; if you don't hand in socks, you don't get any. You're allowed one set if you live on a unit where showers are communal, two sets if the showers are on the block. If it is discovered that you have more, you will likely be given a disciplinary case. It is not unusual for an inmate to be given a major case and lose class, status, and good time for having some extra underwear and socks in his cell. On most units, this exchange, called necessities, is done in a storage room. In others, it's done in the shower room itself. But since all clothes are interchangeable and none of it owned individually, it is a fairly simple process. The laundry will wash the clothes, send it to the necessities department, which will take so many pants of this size, so many of that size, so many shirts, socks, and sets of shorts and exchange them with inmates for their dirty sets on a daily basis, at set times.

Now, for the exceptions. Bleach is used sparingly, and the clothes take on a yellowish tinge after time. Nothing is pressed, and if the necessities department has nothing clean in your size, you have a choice— keep your dirty clothes or wear something that doesn't fit. Some inmates—the waiters and cooks for the Officers' Dining Room, the orderlies in administration, some clerks—are, because of their contact with free-world people or high ranking officers, given their own clothes. Of the same design as other clothes, this clothing is stamped with a red tag that has its owner's name, TDCJ number, and maybe the inmate's housing location. The inmate will be issued four or five sets. They will fit him well and will be ironed for him by inmates in the laundry.

This practice leads to charges of preferential treatment, which are ignored for the most part. All inmates would like pressed clothes, picked to fit well, especially to wear on visiting days. TDCJ considers this a perk that is earned by certain inmates and will continue to ensure that inmates who work around the public or the warden are dressed as well as possible.

Some inmates find a good-fitting set of clothes and hang on to it. They'll buy some bleach from a laundry worker, or buy detergent on the units that stock it, wash the clothes in the toilet or the shower, and press them under their mattress. However, to do this, you must keep an extra set—one to turn in and your good set, called your "tight whites." If a shakedown of your cell turns up an extra set, you will receive a disciplinary case.

The commissary sells thermal underwear, regular tee-shirts, and socks, all in white, of course. If they are altered in any way after being bought— with fancy lettering, cut-off sleeves, etc.—they may be confiscated and the inmate given a case for whatever the confiscating officer may think appropriate. Remember—no individuality.

Shoes of various styles are also sold. Depending on the unit, the commissary will offer cheap tennis shoes, house shoes, and beach-comber sandals for cell and shower use. A few units may sell a type of work boot. Safety rules prohibit the wearing of anything but state-issued boots to work, but units enforce this rule selectively, some allowing commissary-bought shoes to be worn if the job is an inside job that does not require any heavy lifting. A new rule, taking effect in September 2002, limits all inmates to two pairs of shoes—one personal and one TDCJ-issued.

All inmates are given powdered toothpaste and a short-handled toothbrush when they arrive. Almost every unit cuts the handles off any hairbrush and toothbrush, which have been known to be sharpened by some inmates and used as shanks, or homemade knives. This makes it difficult to brush correctly, but it does limit wounds to the length of the cut-off brush handle, usually a couple of inches. This is the only hygiene item inmates will be issued, other than the daily motel-sized soap bar. If inmates want shampoo, deodorant, hair cream, after-shave, or foot powder, all must be bought in the commissary or be done without. Sad, but true.

Inmates are issued one or two razors weekly and must remain clean-shaven. Barbershops are available for haircuts. Some units are more lax than others are, but hair must be kept short—not over the ears, or over the collar. Some inmates—usually the Black inmates who tend to have coarser hair—are given clipper-shave passes. This is done because daily shaving causes them pain and infection from ingrown hairs. This is a genuine problem with many Black inmates, but getting the medical department to approve such a pass, and security to honor it, can be a tremendously frustrating experience.

On older units, showers are communal, accommodating as many as one hundred inmates at one time. You shower when your living quarters are called, or when you come in from work, or you miss showering entirely. Many units shower early in the morning on weekends, between 6 A.M. and 8 A.M. Since inmates are going to be recreating and sweating all day, this makes for some uncomfortable, not to mention smelly situations.

CHAPTER FIVE

work

*I*t comes as a shock to the mostly lazy, unskilled criminals who come into the Texas prison system that, unlike the federal system or most other state prisons, Texas inmates *must* work. *And they do not get paid.* Anything. (More on the financial situation in Chapter nine: Money.) Inside and outside, in snow and rain, day and night, whenever TDCJ needs something done, chances are that an inmate is assigned to do it.

Most inmates who are physically fit are first assigned to work in the fields, in what are called work squads, hoe squads, or sometimes just the Line. The Line is not actually considered a job. It is a way of indoctrinating inmates—especially younger, first-time inmates—to the system, and it is punishment for inmates losing other jobs through disciplinary infractions. Sometimes, it is just punishment for angering the wrong officer.

On most units, the Line does field work. Inmates in the fields plant, weed, thin, and harvest fruits and vegetables. Texas prison crops range from watermelons, peanuts, eggplants, and beets to the more traditional vegetables and, of course, King Cotton.

Inmates in the Line cut trees, break rocks, clean weeds and grass from under miles of fences, and generally work harder than many convicts have ever imagined working in their lives.

Consisting of perhaps fifteen to thirty men, each squad is made up of inmates in a like-custody status. Every squad has one inmate, usually one who has been in the fields a long time, who serves as Lead Row. This inmate sets the pace for various duties as instructed by the squad boss, who is always armed and always on horseback.

The Lead Row also calls the cadence for a particularly brutal exercise called flat-weeding. When flat-weeding, all the inmates in a squad get one behind each other, chest to back, with their hoes held out to the same side. On the command, "Get 'em up!" all hoes are raised head high. On the count of one they come crashing down. Up again, then down on two. Up again, then down on three. Up and down, and on four the whole squad takes a step forward, then repeats the exercise over, over, and over until hands are blistered and bleeding and the ground is broken and the dry clods are dust. Fights break out constantly between inmates irritated by the closeness, the dust and the sheer misery, but too tired to really do anything, the inmates will flail at one another while the rest of the squad appreciates the break. At times, eight or nine squads will be flat-weeding at the same time, a few feet apart, and the sing-song cadences— sometimes truly original and musical, led by the Lead Rows and echoed by the squad—will merge, the thump of hoes sounding a rhythmic counterpoint, and the afternoon will be almost surreal. It gets crazy.

The Line works six to ten hours a day, coming in for lunch. On some units, when summer rolls around and the heat climbs into triple digits, the line will work from 6 A.M. until 12:30 P.M., with hourly water breaks, then come in for that day. The Line is off on weekends and all holidays and usually doesn't work in foggy, wet, or freezing conditions.

Once an inmate has proved himself to be a willing worker, his field boss will recommend him for a job in industry or support services, according to the TDCJ Classification Plan. TDCJ policy when assigning jobs is to try to "match an inmates' skills and experiences with a job that will enhance that inmate's rehabilitative needs without compromising security." What actually happens is that, in most cases, you will be given whatever job is open and needs to be done, given your physical limitations. Whatever skills you have will rust unless there is an urgent need for that particular skill, you do not displease your current supervisor, and you have a semi-clear disciplinary record.

The Texas prison system is run by inmates, but without actual control. All necessary functions of day-to-day operations, including the training of free-world supervisors, are done by inmates. They cook, wash, plant, cultivate, feed, clean, build, weld, paint, etc. The hospital staff and front-office staff are free-world employees, except for the inmate janitors who clean offices. An occasional professional with knowledge in his field may teach his inmate workers, but most TDCJ supervisors are guards who asked for the position, rather than general population guards, and were then taught the intricacies of their jobs by inmates.

I have worked as a data entry operator, a hospital and law library clerk, a gardener, a pot washer, a grill cook—never have I been taught my job by my supervisor. Perhaps the only exceptions to this are the skilled supervisors who work for maintenance, but even then, inmates aren't assigned to work for maintenance unless they have electrical, plumbing, or painting skills to begin with.

Inmates save the system enormous amount of money. On the Wynne Unit, in the Mechanical Department, or transportation, there are approximately sixty mechanics and welders who help keep the TDCJ fleet of buses and trucks running, doing a job for free that would cost the system a minimum of $1.5 million a year, if you assume free-world mechanics would work for an average of thirteen dollars an hour and work forty hours a week. And that's just one unit, in one industry. Inmates on factory-intensive units such as Wynne, Huntsville (the Walls), or Coffield may be assigned to a factory and perform semi- or high-skilled labor. TDCJ factories produce stainless steel products, garments, mattresses, cardboard boxes, furniture, shoes, highway signs, soap, wax, and much more. The system operates canneries, meat cutting plants, textile mills, bus-repair, and records conversion facilities—and all of the actual work is done by inmates.

One negative aspect of this is that there is little accountability demanded from the supervisors. A supervisor who has poor work habits or is simply incompetent is usually propped up by competent workers (inmates), just like in the free-world. But unlike the free-world, a prison supervisor who makes a mistake can place blame on his workers, who dare not contradict his statements. They must accept whatever abuse or charges a supervisor heaps on them, especially if they are at a job that they enjoy, or one that they are attempting to learn well in order to pursue the same job upon release. A supervisor can fire them at will, have them reassigned to the Line or anywhere he wants, and not face any sort of legal action. He does not have to justify the firings to anyone, and with a simple request he can get a new batch of workers. The supply of workers in prison is endless.

Inmates with a more than basic education and a willingness to accept responsibility will eventually work their way into one of the "Cadillac" jobs—library clerk, boiler room operator, kitchen commissary clerk. Those jobs are essential to the running of a unit, and as long as the inmates assigned to those positions don't get too far out of line—no inmate is indispensable, and no job is truly safe—they will essentially be left alone for the length of their sentences. A few jobs that inmates are no longer allowed to hold are front office and infirmary clerking positions. Before *Ruiz*, clerks took count, wrote drug prescriptions, and had access to other inmates' records, and they used that access to blackmail inmates or to run scams on their families or other free-world people. This is now rarely true, or even possible.

Those duties—and any duty that involves handling personal information—are performed by free-world personnel. Clerking positions still exist, but most involve little more than general typing and filing, albeit in comfortable surroundings. Some clerks work on computers and serve as accountants for various industries. No inmate, however, has access to the Internet.

I mentioned physical capabilities being one criteria for job assignments. When an inmate comes through Diagnostic, the medical staff notes any physical infirmities and decides if those infirmities are deserving of entry into an inmate's permanent file. If they are, restrictions may accompany them. For example, an inmate with a bad back may be prohibited from lifting more than twenty pounds, and another may be prohibited from working in direct sunlight due to a skin condition. TDCJ has a mixed record when it comes to honoring these medical restrictions. I've known officers who ignore medical restrictions, order an inmate to perform duties he shouldn't, and then give the inmate a disciplinary case for Refusing to Obey an Order if he doesn't comply, even if physically incapable. Why, you ask, would he do this? Most officers are taught that all inmates are lying in almost every circumstance. If an officer sees something that needs to be done, tells an inmate to do it and the inmate says he has restrictions, the officer may be unwilling to look for another inmate and will simply order the inmate to perform the job or get written up. The officer knows that his ranking officers will back him up. More often than not, the investigating officer will allow the case to be processed, and will tell the inmate that he should have performed the duty and then filed a grievance against the officer. Never mind the fact that actually performing the duty meant the inmate was putting himself at physical risk. (More on the bewildering, frustrating and ultimately self-defeating world of TDCJ rules in chapter seventeen.)

Because many restrictions will prevent their ever being assigned to the Line, inmates have often gone to bizarre lengths to have restrictions placed in their files. While the Line is usually not the exceedingly brutal work it used to be, it is still hard, and for some inmates, terrifying, especially because the field bosses take a casual view of inmates fighting out in the fields. Inmates have intentionally broken their own fingers and severed their own Achilles tendons in order to not be assigned to the fields.

CHAPTER SIX

administrative segregation

*T*here are stories about the new Super-Seg and Super-Max Units, stories that focus on the inhumane aspects of those prisons. Marion in Illinois, Pelican Bay in California—they and the prisons like them are the new Alcatrazes. There the supposedly incorrigible are sentenced to years of subhuman life, their movements dictated by shadows behind unbreakable glass, a red, blinking glare of light sensors admitting them in and out of echoing corridors. These are places where life is twenty-four hours of enforced loneliness. The only human contact allowed is when one is transferred, shackled with leg irons and handcuffs, and in some cases wheeled on a gurney, a mask over one's face, like so much savage freight.

As I write this, there are four super maximum-security prisons in Texas—Estelle, Smith, Clements, and Allred High Security Units. While they are undoubtedly more secure, with unit policies that result in inmates being isolated from each other in ways not possible on other units, the great majority of Texas inmates in ad/seg are on units where the ad/seg wings are part of the general prison, not in the four stand-alone high security units. That is not the case in California, where Pelican Bay is, by policy, practice, and physical attributes, set apart from every other California state prison. The policies that govern Texas ad/seg are the same, whether the ad/seg environment consists of the dilapidated, six by nine feet pre-*Ruiz* cells on Wynne, Eastham, Ellis, Coffield, or other older units; the newer, more spacious ad/seg wings on Robertson, Hughes, Michael, and other pod-like wings built after *Ruiz*; or whether on the four units built specifically as ad/seg units, touted as such by politicians and designed to be more secure, more spartan, and thus more feared. However, after conversations with various inmates who have done time in many ad/seg environments, including the super maximum units, the biggest adjustment (and perhaps the only major difference) is the level of loneliness. On the non-high security units, it is still fairly easy to communicate with other inmates. That is not the case on the new high security units. The level of isolation is such that most of the inmates I've spoken to all agree that merely holding on to one's sanity required a level of strength and inner resources they did not know they had.

Texas practices two types of segregation in its dealing with inmates. One is administrative, and is not so much punishment as it is an assignment. The other is in fact punishment, called punitive segregation, and is the one I'll look at first.

At one time, they called it the Hole, and on some units that's what it was—a hole in the ground. Officials dropped inmates into it and shoved a piece of tin over the opening. In other prisons they put inmates into cages, out where the heat, flies, and rain could make them blister, bleed, and, supposedly, see the error of their ways. It was about punishment, which is after all what "punitive" means. It is also called solitary confinement, and before *Ruiz*, on any officer's whim, an inmate could be stripped naked and thrown into a dark cell for fifteen days at a time. He would shower once a week, if at all, and be denied medical care, mail and visits. He would be fed a few tablespoons of vegetables three times a day and one full meal every third day, and he would emerge having lost up to a pound of weight per day, only to return if staff believed he had not repented and was still a convict with an attitude.

Things have changed. Inmates can still be sentenced to fifteen days of solitary, but now they're weighed before and after, constantly checked by medical personnel, fed three hot meals a day, receive mail, and are allowed access to legal resource material. Visits are still denied to inmates in punitive seg and it is still considered punishment, but only because it signifies that an inmate has been found guilty of a major rule infraction. It is no longer feared. It is not the Hole.

Administrative segregation—commonly referred to as ad/seg—is the end result of a process begun when someone decides that it is best for all concerned that a particular inmate be assigned a cell to himself, kept strictly away from all other inmates, and released back into the general population only after many reviews. According to TDCJ policy, ad/seg is a "non-punitive status involving separation of an offender from the general population for the purpose of maintaining safety, security, and order among the general population offenders and correctional personnel within the prison institution." By policy, "at no time is Administrative Segregation to be used as punishment for misconduct." (Both quotes are from the TDCJ-ID Administrative Segregation Plan, November 1999.)

There is one other crucial difference between the two types of segregation—the due process requirements provided to inmates sent to either. They are much stricter, more detailed, if an inmate is going to punitive segregation. The reasoning here is that since punitive segregation is punishment, with inmates liable to lose good time that could cut their sentences' length, they are entitled to stringent due process requirements to safeguard those "liberty" entitlements. Since ad/seg is not punishment, (at least not in the eyes of those not assigned to ad/seg,) but merely a living assignment, inmates need not be afforded those due process requirements. This argument was waged for years, and finally the Supreme Court weighed in with the definitive word in *Hewitt v. Helms.*

"Owing to the central role of these types of initial judgments, a decision that an inmate or group of inmates represent a threat to the institution's security would not be appreciably fostered by the trial-type procedural safeguards suggested by respondent. This leads us to conclude that the due process clause requires only a informal, non-adversarial review of evidence . . . in order to confine an inmate feared to be a threat to institutional security." (*Hewitt v. Helms,* 103 S. Ct. 864, 1983.)

In case you don't understand what those requirements are, they were specifically spelled out three years later by a lower court: "We specifically find that the due process clause does not require detailed written notice of charges, representation by counsel substitute, an opportunity to present witnesses, or a written decision describing the reasons for placing the prisoner in administrative segregation." (*Toussaint v. McCarthy,* 801 F.2d 1080, 9th Cir. 1986.)

In words that most people will understand—to be assigned to ad/seg, the administration need not tell you why in writing, need not provide you with counsel, does not have to allow you to testify in your behalf, and does not have to allow you to provide witnesses, especially since they don't have to tell you of the charges against you. After all, it is merely another *assignment.*

On a unit level, it takes the recommendation and approval of the unit warden to be assigned to ad/seg. That recommendation must be approved by the Unit Classification Committee and then by the State Classification Committee, both to get assigned to and released from ad/seg.

Assignment to ad/seg is, perhaps not so curiously, desired by some inmates. In Level I of ad/seg, inmates still have their commissary privileges, and they are allowed to buy and possess radios, fans and typewriters. They are single-celled and generally left alone and don't need to worry about the fighting and tension of the general population. They are, however, denied participation in school programs, all drug and alcohol abuse programs, have fewer hours of recreation, no church services, no contact visits, and no social interaction of any kind with other inmates.

But if Level I is a sort of benign isolation, Levels II and III are horrifying in their effect on inmates. Here I will refer to the March 1, 1999, ruling by Judge William Wayne Justice concerning TDCJ's ongoing efforts to prove that the *Ruiz* accords were unnecessary because TDCJ had improved its policies and self-policing to the extent that federal oversight was no longer needed. Judge Justice disagreed, and the following testimony helped convince him.

According to Dr. Craig William Haney, Ph.D., who is the Chairperson of the Psychology Department at the University of California at Santa Cruz, inmates in the lower levels of ad/seg exist in world " in which smeared feces, self-mutilation, and incessant babbling and shrieking are almost daily occurrences." (*Ruiz v. Johnson,* 37 F. Supp. 2d 855, at 910.) Haney testified that he found "high levels of prisoners [who] were living in psychological distress and pain." Dr. Haney said the Texas ad/seg units were "as bad or worse as any I've ever seen." He testified to the circular, self-fulfilling purpose of ad/seg. Inmates are suffering such psychological deprivation, he testified, that their behavior becomes worse and they are less able to conform to prison rules. In his legal analysis and conclusion, Judge Justice stated, "inmates in administrative segregation, particularly those in Levels II and III, are deprived of even the most basic psychological needs. More than mere deprivation, however, these inmates suffer actual psychological harm from their almost total deprivation of human contact, mental stimulus, personal property, and human dignity." (*ibid.* page 913.)

So, if punishment isn't the goal of ad/seg, how do inmates get there, and why? There are generally two types of inmates in ad/seg—those who ask for and are granted protective custody, and those ordered locked up because they are believed to represent a threat to other inmates or staff due to repeated assaults on staff or inmates.

Inmates are assigned to protective custody if they convince staff they will be hurt or killed if left in the general population. The staff does not agree to this out of empathy for inmates. Most officers believe that whatever happens to inmates is justified by their crimes. But if an inmate is killed or severely hurt by other inmates, and if he can prove that TDCJ officials knew of the threat, and it was a particular threat to that particular inmate, and officials did nothing to prevent any ensuing injury or death, then the courts have held that prison administrators, and in some cases individual guards, are liable.

Before an inmate is granted protective custody status, he will need to show evidence of a beating (sometimes a severe one), and be willing to point out those who have beaten him, and prove it will happen again and again unless he is locked away. From the staff's point of view, those steps—a visible beating, willingness to testify and proof of further violence—are necessary, given that the general population is expected to be a violent place, with *all* inmates in imminent danger of beatings.

Add in the fact that all inmates are expected to work hard, and sometimes for long hours, then factor in ad/seg's relatively benign reputation, (in Level I, at least,) and you can almost understand the cynicism. Almost. The truth is, there are many inmates, mostly young and Anglo, who despair of ever proving to staff that the threats, slaps, ass pinchings, and general harassment actually constitute mortal threats. But by the time things escalate to the point of bloody beatings, and they are being called out to defend themselves at work and in the dayrooms every day with the expectation that they will eventually break; many have already given in, submitted to the more aggressive predators and are paying protection or doing whatever it takes to make the pain and fear stop. The truth is that most of the ones who truly need protection are put off by the humiliating steps necessary to be granted it.

There are three quicker, more certain ways to get into ad/seg—assault a guard, attempt to escape, or become a confirmed gang member, especially an Hispanic gang member.

Assaulting staff will get an inmate—along with a good beating in retaliation—into pre-hearing detention, which is similar to ad/seg in that he will have no work assignment and is on lockdown status. The Unit Classification Committee will decide whether or not to recommend him for ad/seg status. If the assault is a one-time affair and not part of a larger violent history, the inmate will lose class, good time, be dropped in custody, and returned to the general population. If he is deemed a threat to staff, he'll remain in lockdown status while the unit's recommendation to place him in ad/seg is reviewed by the state committee, and eventually he'll be segregated.

If an inmate is pegged as a gang member, especially one of the Hispanic gangs that are constantly at war, he will be segregated, most likely for the length of this sentence, or until he thoroughly renounces gang membership. (On the four ad/seg wings I have worked in, Level I was almost entirely composed of confirmed members of Hispanic gangs, most quietly doing their time. Officers who work ad/seg will tell you the same—the least trouble given them is by the Hispanic gang members, who have strict codes that govern them while they are in ad/seg.)

An inmate's level in ad/seg is different from his custody level. *All* ad/seg inmates are treated as maximum, locked down inmates. The ad/seg level—usually determined by an inmate's behavior while in ad/seg—is used to establish what privileges ad/seg inmates are allowed: how much personal property they may possess, how much they can spend at the commissary, whether they are allowed to check out books from the library, whether they are allowed visits.

Ad/seg inmates never leave their cells without being handcuffed and/ or leg-chained. They are fed the same as the general population, except that their food is brought to them. If they throw food at the guards, they will be fed food loaf. Ad/seg inmates are allowed a pre-determined number of hours of weekly recreation, almost always alone, unless they are known to be members of the same gang. They are allowed to request books from the library and legal materials from the law library, and depending on their ad/seg level and the warden's policy, are allowed to study via correspondence and to do some limited in-cell piddling (see chapter fourteen). They are reviewed every three to six months for possible upgrades in level and in custody.

Overall, life in ad/seg is the worst existence possible for an inmate. Once in, it is extremely difficult to get out. If you know anyone in ad/ seg, you should make every effort to convince him to do all he can to be allowed back into the general population. If that is not possible, you should do everything you can to ensure he is surviving—write often, visit, and call the warden frequently to put him on notice that you care for that inmate.

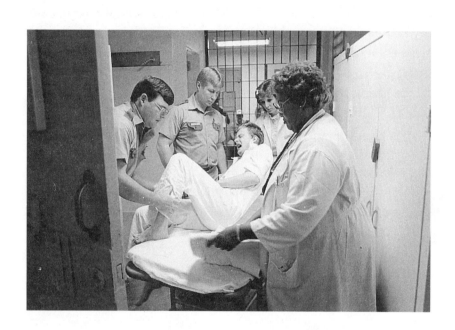

CHAPTER SEVEN

medical and dental facilities

Because the medical care received in prison is such an important issue, this chapter is broken into two parts. The second, Appendix B, is taken word-for-word from the TDCD-ID Comprehensive Health Manual, and it outlines what services are available to Texas inmates. As you will see, they are impressive and are an enormously welcome improvement from the shockingly negligent system in place before *Ruiz.*

However, there is a huge gulf between what services are available and what services are actually provided. Many factors influence the quality of prison medicine, and the single biggest is the attitude I referred to in chapter one—the system cares little for inmates' welfare except when it is possible that staff negligence may result in an inmate's injury and death, and the system will then be held liable.

In this chapter I will again refer to Judge Justice's March 1, 1999 order in *Ruiz v. Johnson,* 37 F. Supp 2d and 55 (S. D. Tex. 1999.) While Judge Justice did not find the medical practices unconstitutional, the testimony of expert and inmate witnesses, and the admissions of medical personnel and TDCJ officials, will help illustrate some of the problems I will point out.

In 1994, the Legislature created the six-member Correctional Managed Health Care Advisory Committee (currently nine members) to take over management of TDCJ's health care delivery system. Through this process, the day-to-day operations of the medical system are assumed by the University of Texas Medical Branch (UTMB) at Galveston and the Texas Tech Health Science Center. What this means is that TDCJ is merely a conduit between the health care providers and the inmates themselves.

From an inmate's point of view, the medical system is simple. An inmate who is sick or has a medical or dental problem requests to be seen by filling out a sick call slip. The nursing staff will evaluate the nature and severity of the complaint and schedule the inmate to be seen. He will come in, his vital signs taken and recorded (weight, temperature, and blood pressure,) and he will explain the exact nature of his problem to the nurse. She or he will then decide what is needed, and if a doctor's opinion is believed necessary, she will schedule an appointment.

There are many inmates who undoubtedly abuse the medical procedures. They wish to miss work and thus they exaggerate their problems. They may want to be reassigned to another job, or to another unit. They may be attempting to be prescribed certain drugs to feed a habit. They may simply want to sit in the air-conditioned waiting room and ogle the nurses. Inevitably, the nursing staff will begin to think of inmates as malingering liars instead of patients. This view is worsened by the fact that actual access to any unit infirmary is controlled by TDCJ officers, who open the doors, lock the doors, lock inmates into the waiting rooms, and sit with them, and by their presence ensure that the often unruly inmates maintain a respectful attitude toward the nurses. However, unless an inmate is bleeding or has some outward sign of illness, most officers will believe the sickness is faked.

This attitude pervades every step of TDCJ medical care. It afflicts the nursing staff and security, and since no inmate moves in prison without security's blessing, minor ailments are ignored and become major, at which point the inmate's health has deteriorated and thousands of dollars must be spent attacking what was preventable if not for someone's assumption that the inmate was lying.

A complete compendium of the problems bedeviling the TDCJ health-care system would take chapters. I will merely quote some of the more relevant passages in *Ruiz v. Johnson.*

John M. Robertson, M.D., M.P.H., is the Health Services Bureau Chief and Medical Director for the New Mexico Corrections Department. He is a full faculty member at the University of New Mexico in the department of medicine. Dr. Robertson was one of the primary expert witnesses in *Ruiz v. Johnson*, and he spent more than three hundred hours "evaluating the quality of medical care in TDCJ by analyzing the data culled from death charts of 59 inmates who died in 1998." (page 894, *Ruiz v. Johnson.*) In his summary "Summary Findings," he reported:

> "This review of deaths presents a troubling pattern of systemic problems in the health care delivery to inmates in the Texas Department of Criminal Justice. Of a total of fifty-nine charts reviewed, twenty (34%) were found to have received poor to very poor medical care. To assure that this finding was balanced, a very conservative approach was taken, namely, only when a significant clinical outcome could be demonstrated was a score lower than three (below satisfactory) given. Of particular concern was the finding that sixteen of the deaths (twenty-seven per cent) could be deemed as "preventable." Among the potentially preventable deaths, nine of sixteen had serious concerns regarding oversight and/or follow-up while seven of the forty-three deaths that were not evaluated as preventable demonstrated the same deficits." (*ibid,* page 895.)

The testimony presented was rife with instances of non-physicians making decisions beyond their expertise; of inadequate evaluations and referrals; of failures to follow up on patients who were defined as "at-risk"; of staff indifference; of poor communication between work assignments, where security officers ordered inmates to perform duties prohibited by medical restrictions.

Some of the more glaring examples of the above were:

1. Inmate Arthur Heinz at Garza West died after repeatedly returning to the infirmary with highly elevated blood pressure. He was only allowed to see nurses for half his visits. He died of cardiac arrest five days later.

2. Inmate Jason Wimberly visited medical personnel five times in a day and a half with what Dr. Robertson asserts were obvious signs of appendicitis. He was not seen by a doctor, and the nurses who evaluated him did not recognize the symptoms. On the fifth visit, the inmate was rushed to the hospital with a perforated, gangrenous appendix.

3. William Bishop's broken arm went untreated for two weeks at the Hughes Unit.

4. Ala Mae Jacobson waited two weeks for treatment of her broken wrist.

5. A growing mass in inmate Gilberto Cristo's lung was not diagnosed, despite a number of x-rays, until it was inoperable metastatic cancer.

6. One patient was diagnosed as having a possible life-threatening growth in his kidney and was scheduled for surgery in two or three weeks, but was not sent for the procedure for six months, by which time the growth had led to metastatic disease. He died.

7. Inmate Colling Gentry showed obvious symptoms of an acute heart attack but was sent back to his cell.

8. Michael Bias, who fell into a coma after a suicide attempt, was left to lie in one position for so long that he developed infected pressure sores that led to massive loss of skin, breakdown of muscle, and kidney failure.

9. Ophelia Rangel spent five days not eating. Suffering from psychotic episodes and severe diarrhea, she was not treated. She died.

10. Robert Lee was diagnosed by a physician's assistant as "malingering." The inmate became paralyzed and was sent to emergency radiation therapy to regain control of his legs and bladder.

In the worst cases, the disparities between treatment in the hospital and in the prison unit seems to have been not the result of miscommunication, but of unit-based doctors ignoring the recommendations made at the hospitals. (*ibid,* page 900.)

Other times, the "communication" problems seemed to be between medical staff and security staff. There were numerous inmates whose medically based work restrictions were apparently ignored by officers on the units and in the field squads. (This echoes what I said in chapter five about security ignoring medical restrictions.) Inmate Alfa Turner testified about being made to lift heavy objects after her wrist surgery. One inmate was misassigned to work in the fields despite a drug regimen that prohibited such duties. The inmate received disciplinary cases for refusing to work. Two weeks after a psychologist wrote a memorandum to the unit warden about the problem, the inmate had a stroke-like episode in the fields.

The TDCJ doctors and administrators who testified in the civil action admitted that they knew of only one security officer who had ever been disciplined for violating policy against assigning inmates to duties that clashed with medical restrictions, pointing out the almost uncorrectable flaw in the entire system—great policy but terrible practice allowed by superior officers.

In sum, "large numbers of inmates throughout the TDCJ system are not receiving adequate health care." (*ibid,* page 906.) But, as Judge Justice noted, "although it is found that medical and psychiatric care systems in TDCJ are frequently found grossly wanting, and that plaintiffs may have in fact shown deliberate indifference to individual cases or institutions, it cannot be stated, under present-day law, that TDCJ officials are systemically and deliberately indifferent to inmates' medical and psychiatric needs." Thus, TDCJ does not violate inmates' constitutional rights with its role in the managed health care system, one, which, while at times grossly negligent, is much better than the one prior to *Ruiz v. Estelle.*

Inmates are now required by law to pay three dollars for any visit they request to the infirmary, unless it is: 1) in response to an emergency situation; 2) initiated by the department; 3) initiated by the health-care provider; 4) consists of routine follow-up, prenatal, or chronic care; or 5) provided under a contractual obligation that is established under the Interstate Corrections Compact or under an agreement with another state that precludes assessing a co-payment.

According to state law, the TDCJ may not deny an inmate access to health care as a result of the inmate's failure or inability to make a co-payment. This three-dollar fee, and the managed health care system in general, have resulted in a firestorm of controversy since their inception. Some inmates and their families have charged that the managed health care providers, like some providers in the free-world, are cutting corners by providing minimal care and giving bonuses to physicians and nurses allowing them to do so. I urge relatives and friends of inmates to remain aware of the possibilities for abuse.

Prior to the three-dollar co-payment, Texas inmates could not buy any sort of preventive medicine. We were not allowed aspirin, cough syrup, analgesics, antihistamines, pain-relieving ointments—anything of that nature. *If* we were in possession of anything that had not been prescribed to us, or in excess of amounts of medications authorized, we would receive disciplinary cases.

The system now sells inmates with money the following over-the-counter medications in the commissary: antacid, analgesics, antihistamines, cough syrups, cortisone cream, nasal spray, antibiotic ointment, and hemorrhoid ointment. But if you can't afford medicine, and you must go to the infirmary for your medication, you have a choice to make. If you have a cold, you can't fight it. You can't buy orange juice, cold tablets, or cough syrup, or stay at home and drink chicken soup. You must request to be seen by the nurse and run the risk of her telling you there is nothing wrong with you and prescribing two Tylenol tablets, for three dollars. You can ignore it, hope it goes away and if it doesn't, put in a request after it has worsened. Your request will be answered and you will be called in when you are all but recovered. By then, the whole block is sniffling and facing the same dilemma.

Most winters are cycles of misery in prison, because the system makes it so difficult for inmates to receive anything that would lessen the chance of spreading the cold or flu. Since we are not allowed to adequately treat colds ourselves, and we know how the system works, we ignore minor symptoms until they become major. There is no such thing as calling in sick or not reporting to work. Unless the medical department has issued a valid lay-in, the inmate must report to work, even if he has a temperature of 103° and is coughing terribly. Of course, he will then spread his disease to other inmates.

There exists a walk-in procedure for inmates who insist they are sick enough to be escorted to the infirmary and cannot wait for the procedure to run its course. They must badger whichever officer is on duty, risking being written up for "Creating a Disturbance." But if they persist, an officer will eventually call the medical department, tell them he has an inmate who claims he has a medical emergency, and put the ball in the medical department's court. Usually, the infirmary will ask the officer if the inmate has visible signs of sickness, in effect asking the untrained guard to diagnose the inmate. Depending on the officer's disposition and his relationship with the inmate, he may or may not tell the infirmary that the inmate indeed looks ill. If not, the infirmary will advise the inmate to send in a sick call request.

It is often easier for a supervisor at work to escort an inmate to the infirmary, because the supervisor has a better idea if that particular inmate is a malingerer, or an inmate who, through his work habits and behavior, is one whose word can be trusted. Indeed, many supervisors take it on themselves to bring in small items of medication for their workers and will tell an inmate to go to his cell if he looks sick.

Real emergencies in prison take on a surreal aspect. Inmates sometimes thrash around on the floor, suffering from heart attacks, epileptic seizures, or stab wounds; other inmates offer commentary; officers shuffle to and fro; and nurses slowly push a gurney down the hallway, evidently believing that the situation is not an emergency and if it is, a few minutes more won't hurt.

Another problem that hampers TDCJ medical care is that officers are required to fill out accident reports if an inmate injures himself then reports it to the officer and demands to be taken immediately to the infirmary. TDCJ policy requires inmates to inform someone whenever they are injured, either on the job, on the yard, or in the cell. Policy also requires that officers are to file injury reports and are never to attempt to evaluate medical problems. However, to avoid paperwork, many officers will tell the injured inmates that if he insists on seeing a nurse immediately, the officer will write the inmate a disciplinary case for Committing an Unsafe Act. Many inmates will call the officer's bluff. Some will try to care for themselves, resulting in the condition becoming worse. When they finally do go to sick call, they must lie about the initial incident, because the officer will probably deny his part in it, and the inmate is liable to receive a disciplinary case anyway for not reporting the initial incident.

AIDS in Prison

Between 1990 and 1998, AIDS (Acquired Immune Deficiency Syndrome) killed 703 inmates in TDCJ. It is by far the deadliest killer in prison. A report by the United Nations Program on HIV/AIDS, quoted by the Center for Disease Control's National Clearinghouse, says that "the numbers of HIV-infected prisoners is in some cases up to ten times the level seen in local populations. Prisons offer ideal conditions for the spread of the virus, including intravenous drug use, tattooing, sexual tension, and an atmosphere of fear and violence."

To make matter worse, a recent study by Dr. Michael O'Brien of the University of Texas Medical Branch at Galveston (UTMB) showed some Texas prisoners were infected with a form of the virus resistant to the newest and most successful medicines used to fight it. Not only were Texas inmates infected with the drug-resistant form of HIV—inmates became infected while in prison.

Resistance to medication can occur when patients do not take pills as prescribed. Inmates, unlike free-world patients, are not allowed to manage their own medication regimen. Inmates may not make a "pill call" due to many reasons—a lack of escort officers, "rack-ups" due to count time foul ups, or by merely sleeping through the only time pills are passed out. In some cases, the stigma attached to being HIV positive may compel some inmates to refuse medication while still continuing their high-risk behavior.

Another UTMB researcher feared that prison's hothouse atmosphere was breeding more disease. Dr. Richard Pollard, who took part in the UTMB study, recommended that better AIDS education among TDCJ inmates was necessary. He advocated issuing condoms and sterile needles to Texas inmates.

At this time, the best guess is that there are from 7,000 to 12,000 men and women in TDCJ with HIV/AIDS. TDCJ tested 49,000 inmates in

1998, the majority of them incoming inmates. (TDCJ does not require testing. It asks all incoming inmates if they wish to be tested and tests those who wish it, and also offers anonymous testing to all TDCJ inmates.) Of the 49,000, 971 tested positive, reflecting the lower infection rate of incoming prisoners. There were 2,393 prisoners known to be infected in TDCJ in 1998. If fears are accurate and if the infection rate is ten times the local rate, then when one factors in the untested 100,000 prisoners, the numbers of infected inmates may reach five figures.

That number will grow, because the proliferation of homosexual sex in prison guarantees the spread of AIDS. Homosexual sex is extremely common in prison. There are not only the self-admitted homosexuals, many of whom sell their sexual favors, but there exists a large group of "turnouts," or men who have been coerced into sex. These men have no choice with whom they have sex. They are bought and traded. One turnout may have sex with a hundred men, and if one carries the HIV virus, the consequences could be disastrous.

TDCJ does little to combat this. Each unit has a nurse who is designated the Coordinator of Contagious/Infectious Diseases (CID), whose purpose seems to be to give each inmate a tuberculosis (TB) test once a year. Inmates are not given yearly physical examinations. The system may claim otherwise, but from 1992 through 2001 I was called to the infirmary five times, all to be given TB tests. Never did I have any blood drawn, any x-rays taken; I was not pushed, poked, prodded, or asked any questions by a doctor or nurse, except in response to my requests.

The CID is the originator of any information on infectious diseases, which means she will hand a pamphlet to an inmate if he asks for one. Nothing is done to prevent the spread of any disease—no written material is presented to the inmate population, there are no discussions offered, and the only prescription against the high-risk behavior that contributes to AIDS is of a highly punitive nature.

This may change. In a recent conversation with the TDCJ Director of Preventative Health and the TDCJ Director of Health Services, the two officials seemed sincere in their desires to address the AIDS problem. They claimed that they were trying to initiate volunteer-led programs to teach core groups of convicts about AIDS prevention and spread, and have those groups talk to the population in general. They were also open to TDCJ offering educational videos through its television system, with programming scheduled on certain times throughout the system. It remains to be seen if any of these programs are implemented.

If an inmate tests positive for HIV, he remains assigned to population, with regular jobs and programming as his health and behavior warrant. An attempt is made to provide him with single celling, or with multiple cell housing with another inmate who has a blood borne disease. If an inmate has full-blown AIDS and meets certain criteria, he will be transferred to a unit designated for similar inmates.

A recent problem in TDCJ is the alarming prevalence of Hepatitis C. It is estimated that a quarter of the inmates in TDCJ have this virus, which may result in death, albeit decades away, from liver damage. The high-risk population for Hepatitis C is intravenous drug users, alcohol abusers, and those receiving tattoos—and a large percentage of TDCJ inmates fall into those categories. The system is hammering out a policy in an attempt to deal with this crisis. In fact, it seems to be more concerned with this than with AIDS, perhaps because AIDS is contracted by inmates involved in activities TDCJ denies exist within the system and for which it has no coherent policy—homosexual sex and IV drug abuse.

A few final thoughts on medical care in TDCJ. Although Judge Justice did not find overall medical care in the system to be unconstitutional, he did find the psychiatric care in ad/seg in violation. It has been estimated that up to ten percent of prisoners in TDCJ—at least 14,000—are suffering from acute mental illness. If these inmates do not identify themselves as mentally ill, they run the risk of being mislabeled as disciplinary problems instead of medical ones and of spiraling into what one expert call the "tragic, vicious cycle" of despair.

Dr. Terry Kupers, a psychiatrist who has co-chaired the Committee on the Mentally Ill Behind Bars of the American Association of Community Psychiatrists, in his book *Prison Madness*, describes the cycle. A man is identified as disturbed. His freedom is constricted and he is denied certain means of self-expression. He acts out and is placed under tighter security constraints after the staff decides his outbursts reflect "badness" instead of "madness," and should be punished instead of treated. He ends up, more often than not, in ad/seg.

"At each step along the way," Kupers writes, "the correctional staff thinks their earlier assumption about just how bad this prisoner really is has been borne out by this new example of recalcitrance and disrespect of authority. Meanwhile, the prisoner is more convinced he is being disrespected and abused, he becomes even angrier and he is even less willing or able to follow the incrementally stricter rules." (Kupers, 1999, 55.)

Once in ad/seg, the picture is bleak. Dr. Craig Haney, Ph.D., Chair of the Psychology at the University of California at Santa Cruz and according to *Ruiz* trial transcripts "perhaps the nation's leading expert in the area of penal institution psychology," testified not only to the debilitating effects of ad/seg but specifically addressed conditions in TDCJ ad/seg units. Dr. Haney reiterated what Kupers had described—a tragic, vicious cycle. He testified that inmates in ad/seg suffer such psychological deprivation that their behavior becomes worse and they become less able to conform to prison rules. Another expert witness—Dr. Dennis Michael Jurczak, Chief of Neuropsychiatry at the U.S. Naval Hospital—testified that there "was something desperately wrong with a system that would have people this ill sitting in segregation and not being recognized by the mental health staff as needing assistance." (*Ruiz v. Johnson*, 37 F. Supp. 2nd 855 at 912.)

TDCJ and the legislators who lobbied for and appropriated the funds to build the super-seg units dispute that there are inmates in ad/seg other than those who willfully committed actions to land them there—the "worst of the worst." I leave this to your own conclusions.

With the longer sentences being passed for more convicts, there will come a day when the prison population will contain a large number of senior citizens. The system does a commendable job with them now. Many are assigned to a unit that has a wing similar to a nursing home for the aged, cared for by inmates who have volunteered for and been trained in that area.

However, many of those inmates will die in prison, and a better job could be done to make their last years more dignified. It will be up to the public to ensure that older convicts be allowed a chance to contribute—either to the local community or to the prison community—and make these geriatric units and hospices other than places where men sit around waiting to die.

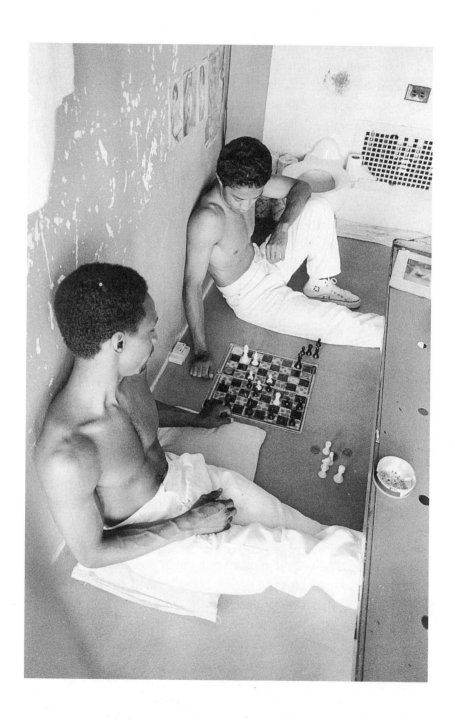

CHAPTER EIGHT

recreation

TDCJ considers anything an inmate does out of his cell to be recreation, unless it is chow or part of his officially assigned duties. The official terms for recreation are either "programmatic activities," which includes all officially sanctioned group meetings, and "non-programmatic activities," which is essentially everything else.

Inmates spend most of their time at work, in their cells or socializing in the dayrooms or on the yard. Dayrooms are communal living areas. On most units, they open at 8 A.M. and close at 10:30 P.M. on weekdays and at 1 A.M. on weekends and holidays. They are open all day and are usually noisy and full of inmates. Most dayrooms have from four to ten tables, which seat four; from one bench to four, which seat from five to ten inmates; and have one or two televisions. Depending on the warden's preferences, programs offered on television will range from the basic four networks to ESPN, USA, and various movie channels.

The newer, pod units have larger dayrooms and fewer people per pod, so they usually have only one television. As a result, to allow inmates a choice—and to prevent fights over one group controlling the viewing—prison officials may allow inmates to go from pod to pod on minimum-security wings. When this is the case, one dayroom will be designated a sports dayroom, one a movie dayroom, and one open to voting. According to policy, every program is to be voted on. All televisions are controlled remotely, by the rover, the officer on the floor who controls the remote. There have been innumerable fights and quite a few riots started by one group of inmates refusing to allow another group to watch what they want. Usually, this friction arises between Black and Hispanic groups wanting to see programming that appeals to them.

On many units, the dayroom seating is rigidly enforced by inmates, and it is segregated along racial and geographical lines. Blacks from Dallas will sit on one bench, Chicanos from San Antonio on another. If an inmate sits where he is not supposed to, he faces a beating from his homeboys for placing them under undue pressure by disrespecting the owners of that bench. On some units, an inmate does not sit anywhere but the floor until he proves willing to fight for the privilege of sitting on a bench.

Inmates may check out various table games, which include Scrabble, chess, checkers and dominoes. Some units allow inmates to improvise their own games, and you'll see crude versions of Monopoly, Trivial Pursuit, and other games floating around. The units for males do not allow cards, because it is assumed they would gamble, which of course would lead to fights. This ignores the fact that inmates gamble on almost everything else, but allowing men cards would amount to giving gambling a green light, so the system continues to deny them.

Inmates do not have televisions in their cells, except on Ramsey I and the Walls in Huntsville. Those two units do not have dayrooms, and to build dayrooms would entail huge problems. In order to not close the units down entirely, TDCJ prefers to issue televisions to those inmates.

Inmates go to the dayrooms at the times allowed by the officers, as determined by unit policy. We do not have keys to our cell doors (except, again, for the inmates at the Walls and at Ramsey I.) We cannot open our cells as we see fit, except for a few units that have a tradition of free access. The officers who control the different living quarters will run what are called "in-and-outs," at times they decide, again as determined by unit policy, and at those times inmates can exit or enter the dayrooms from their cells.

In-and-outs are enormously frustrating to inmates, because on most units, they may be hours apart. On older units, dayrooms are not equipped with toilet facilities, except for urinals. Also, an inmate who does not want to stay in the dayroom may come from work, have just missed an in-and-out, and be forced to wait in a crowded dayroom, with no place to sit, for over an hour. Inmates waste hours every day, weeks every year, just waiting for the officers to roll the doors and let them into their cells. That problem is not faced by inmates living in dorms, who can walk to the dayroom-part of the dorm and back whenever they please. It's a trade-off—if you want the privacy a cell affords, you put up with the crowded dayrooms and frustration of in-and-outs.

A large population of inmates do put up with those frustrations, because as crowded and noisy and hot as they are, dayrooms (and rec yards) are our social arenas. They are where we go to meet one another, a place to get away from the emptiness of the echoing cells, with their accusatory blankness and sameness.

But some men do their sentences in the dayrooms, and these men fall into three groups: 1) Hard-core television watchers, who are usually seated directly under the TV, coffee cup and bag of cookies within easy reach, TV Guides in their lap. There is a running joke in Texas prisons that most television fans can recite every line of every Clint Eastwood movie ever made, because invariably they will be voted in. Rarely are Discovery, PBS, History Channel, or any similar shows voted in. The main fare is movies, sports, and, during the daytime, soap operas. 2) Domino players, either gambling or merely passing time. Inmates take their dominoes seriously, slamming the dominoes to the table often. They loudly bemoan their bad luck, their opponent's good luck, or just the general attributes of anyone standing around watching. The domino-playing group is roundly detested by almost every other dayroom group for its high-decibel atmosphere. 3) The socializers, usually homeboys who appropriate a bench or table for themselves. They will share food, pass around photo albums, or just reminiscence about a common memory, arguing if this club was on that street, or who really caused whose divorce back in the 'hood.

In short, dayrooms are where many inmates do time, surrounded by the day-in, day-out familiarity of the known. But frequenting dayrooms can be deadly, literally and metaphorically. Riots begin there, as the crowded, noisy conditions often birth small incidents of casual disrespect. Magnified by the knowledge that many eyes are watching and evaluating, these incidents can blow up into major confrontations. The routine of the dayrooms can also be death to ambition and initiative. Most college students, serious writers, or readers rarely frequent the dayrooms, because only in their cell can they find the solitude and quiet needed for such pursuits.

Every unit also has outside recreation, the hours for which vary enormously from unit to unit, according to the warden's whims, available personnel to monitor the yard, and the weather. Under *Ruiz,* all inmates are to be allowed a minimum amount of hours of recreation inside and outside. (See Appendix E for details.) How that is provided, and whether more is allowed, is up to the warden. Some units have an open recreation policy, called free access, for minimum custody inmates. Under free access, unless it is count time or chow time, any inmate not working is allowed to come and go to recreation as he pleases. Other units severely restrict rec. They may allow inmates outside for an hour at a time, a living section at a time, and rotate times of access.

Some units have a policy that is followed by all shifts, while some have chaos and inconsistency, which is hugely frustrating to inmates with rigid schedules—work at this time, eat at this time, sleep at this time.

For example, during the four years I was on the Robertson Unit, afternoon rec would be called at noon. Although the yard was technically open until 4 P.M., it was almost impossible to go out at any other time because the officers working the block would assume that since the control desk was not actually calling for rec, they did not have to let inmates go. You went at noon or didn't go at all. As a result, you had empty yards and dayrooms full of angry inmates.

On Wynne, on the other hand, afternoon rec hours were the same as Robertson—noon until 4 P.M. But officers on Wynne called rec at noon, at 1 P.M., at 2 P.M., and at 3 P.M. Inmates knew this, could depend on it and could plan on going out when their schedule allowed.

Inmates may be strip searched entering and leaving the rec yards, especially medium and close custody inmates, and likely all inmates on the newer, pod-type units. Since many inmates congregate there, the yards are where many of the riots in TDCJ take place. Inmates of different custody levels generally do not live together and thus do not recreate together. Rec times for medium and close custody inmates are less than minimum, as the appendix on rec shows.

All outside rec yards in TDCJ have at least a basketball half-court, a handball court, a volleyball net, and a weight machine. There may be more—two full-length basketball courts, two handball courts, a baseball field—but all will have the first four. Games are usually informal, and rules are playground: next up keeps score and officiates. The equipment in the gyms is the same as that on the outside yards, except that gyms also have ping pong tables. The gyms are also where a unit that allows inmates to lift free weights keeps the weights and offers workout sessions. In order to be allowed to lift weights, inmates must be minimum custody, maintain a clear disciplinary record, be in good physical condition and be approved by medical staff.

Once upon a time, TDCJ allowed inter-unit competitions in many sports—softball, basketball, volleyball, handball, weight lifting, Ping-Pong, and various domino games. The best in each sport were spotted by staff, nurtured by unit coaches, and coddled by wardens as a way of gaining bragging rights among units. Members of the unit teams were usually assigned to cushy jobs—mostly to the gym or yard itself, where they did little but recreate their sentence away. Participants in the inter-unit competitions would be bused to the hosting units for all-day tournaments, with perhaps hundreds of inmates from many units competing. That once plum opportunity for an athlete to display his skills on a more than unit level is no longer offered. The reforms instituted by *Ruiz,* insisting that all inmates be afforded the same opportunities, along with fears that gang animosities would explode during the tournament, put an end to system-wide competition. Units now offer only intra-unit tournaments, usually on holidays, where inmates are given the chance to compete in the traditional sports for ribbons and certificates.

Some sports festivals are more elaborate than others are. Depending on the initiative of the unit coaches and the flexibility of the wardens, a Fourth of July SportsFest may offer sprints, relays, egg tossings, team sports, dominoes, Scrabble, chess, and other table-game competitions.

An inmate band may set up on the yard, play rock, country, and rhythm and blues favorites, while hot dogs and soft drinks are distributed to inmates and participating staff members. Or, a tournament may offer only basketball, volleyball, and handball competitions, and forget about the other stuff. Regardless of the scope of a unit's tournaments, inmates compete ferociously, usually with little violence, and they treasure the ribbons awarded. They know, as TDCJ administrators know, that the ribbons reward discipline and talent, and they realize that recreation is invaluable as a way of releasing the tensions of prison. They know that without rec, a prisoner would likely explode with pent-up energy. That is why the political grandstanding to do away with prison rec programs is ignored by prison administrators everywhere. Recreation restriction—more accurately, a restriction to one's cell or cubicle except when one is at work or at chow—is imposed for minor rule violations and may last from ten to ninety days.

CHAPTER NINE

money

*L*et's talk about what got many of us in prison: money.

First, TDCJ inmates are not paid. No matter how hard we work, for how many years, we do not receive a penny. Various groups have tried to convince Texas lawmakers to pay inmates a tiny daily stipend. Texas is one of only two or three states that does not pay its inmates. But it takes a courageous legislator to tell his constituents, "Yes, I know these guys robbed and raped and sold drugs and carjacked—I still think we need to pay them."

The legislator might be risking political suicide before he could explain the benefits of making sure that by paying inmates, you could ensure that many don't come back. That would make paying inmates cost efficient, on both monetary terms and humanitarian grounds, because many of us would then not commit the murders and robberies that leave so many innocent victims in our wake. But those benefits are lost in the hazy, blood-red world created by prosecutors bent on convictions now in exchange for misery later.

Let me explain. If you lock up a man for years on end, deny him a chance to use his skills or learn new ones, impress upon him that he is basically a life-long loser, then release him back into society without social skills, coping skills, relationship skills, and with fifty dollars in his pocket: you are sorely mistaken if you believe that man, especially if he has no family to help, will be able to stay afloat and find a place in society.

How will he buy food, clothes, pay two months rent—even two weeks rent plus a deposit—or have any money for a bus in order to go looking for a job, much less get to one, if he's lucky enough to find one?

The exceptional man may overcome these problems. But there are few exceptional men in prison, and even they need to eat. Texas could pay inmates one dollar a day; keep a quarter for a fund to pay victims of violent crime; charge inmates a quarter for rent; put aside a quarter to be paid to that inmate upon his release; and give him a quarter for his occasional purchases in the prison store. In five years, that inmate would have a little over four hundred and fifty dollars awaiting him; in ten years, almost one thousand. It may not seem like much, but it's more than zero he has awaiting him now, and it could make a world of difference to the inmate on his own, trying to succeed. If he does less than five years, chances are he has not yet been institutionalized, has retained skills, has family support, and is not much of a threat to society, not yet. It is the long-term convict, the older inmate, who needs the assistance. For every inmate who does not return, Texas saves thirty thousand dollars a year, the amount the state claims it costs to incarcerate that inmate. And of course, for every inmate who makes it on parole, there is at least one less victim.

But that's in the future, if ever. Today, for an inmate to have money, it must be mailed from the outside. It is deposited in the Inmate Trust Fund, a non-interest bearing account. Every inmate has an account, under his TDCJ number. He is allowed to spend a certain amount every two weeks. (See chart in Appendix D.) He can spend it all at one time, in one trip to the commissary, or depending on how often a unit allows inmates to go to the store—some allow almost unlimited trips, some only one trip a week—he can spend as little as he wants.

Inmates are not allowed cash. *Do not ever send cash* to inmates or try to give them cash. If inmates have cash they will be charged with major disciplinary infractions and be severely disciplined. If you wish to send an inmate money, buy a money order. Postal money orders are the best, although any money order from a reputable business will work. *Do not* make the money order out to the inmate. Make it out to the Inmate Trust

Fund. Put the inmate's name and TDCJ number in the blank that says "For" or, if by chance the money order has no such blank, write the inmate's name and TDCJ number on a prominent spot on the money order. *Do not* mail the money order to the inmate. If you do, it will be returned to you. Mail the money order to: Inmate Trust Fund, P.O. Box 60, Huntsville, TX 77342-0060. Inmates can provide you with deposit forms, which are available to them or to you when you visit. However, it is not necessary that money orders to the trust fund be accompanied by deposit slips. If you mail a money order in the fashion I've described, the money will be deposited in an inmate's account in seven to ten days.

Be smart. Keep the receipt. Things happen, and you may have to trace the money order or prove that you mailed it. TDCJ officials have been convicted of embezzling Inmate Trust Fund monies, just as have officials of banking institutions everywhere. Keep something for your records.

How does an inmate spend his money? Texas prisons give inmates identification cards that are similar to ATM cards. When we go to the store, we give our card to the commissary officer, who runs it through a slot attached to a video terminal. All sorts of information pops up, including that inmate's trust fund balance. If he has funds in his account, and he is not on restriction, and if he has not spent his allotted funds for that time period, and if it is his scheduled day and time to go to the store, he will be allowed to make purchases.

What are inmates allowed to buy? Prison commissaries are small and offer less than the average convenience store. Food, hygiene products, and writing materials make up the bulk of commissary sales. Fans, radios, typewriters, and hot pots are also sold. The single biggest selling items, in terms of money spent, may be either correspondence supplies—stamps and stamped envelopes—and bags of coffee. Both are money substitutes. Inmates buy and sell contraband by putting so many bags or so many stamps on the table. Bets are made in bags and stamps, and payoffs are made in bags and stamps. One bag of coffee may go through five inmates and never be opened.

Here's some advice. If you send money, try to send the same amount the same time of the month. Inmates have no way of knowing their balance, short of asking the commissary officer to check. On many units, doing so is considered a "run," or a trip to the store, and on units that allow only one run per week, a card check on Monday means no commissary for a week.

"So what? How is that a problem?" you may ask. In TDCJ, we can't just go up to the store and point to items. We must have a list, detailing exactly what we want. We are not allowed to make substitutions. The lines are long. The inmates, and the commissary employees, are impatient. If someone writes an inmate and says, "I'm sending you thirty dollars," that inmate is expecting thirty dollars, and does not know the money order is still sitting on the refrigerator. The inmate has only three dollars and gets sent away from the commissary. It is tremendously frustrating. But if the inmate knows you send thirty dollars the first of every month, he can plan, and he can go on the fifteenth of each month with relative certainty that the money will be there. Many inmates are ashamed to ask for money. It isn't necessary to have money to survive in prison. The inmate will eat. He will have clothes; he will not freeze. However, he will stink, have dandruff, nasty teeth, be hungry, never eat a candy bar, or drink a soda. A little money makes the time bearable.

Inmates can be put on restriction for up to ninety days, and during those periods they are allowed to buy only one each of certain hygiene items every thirty days. If an inmate loses his identification card, or if the magnetized strip goes bad and he needs a new card, he is in trouble if he wants to make store. He can fill out a withdrawal slip, thumbprint it and take it to the commissary, but it may take up to eight weeks before it is approved and he is allowed to buy anything. By that time, he may have a new card. That same method—withdrawal slipping—is used by inmates to order books and magazines if they have the money and patience to order them.

If an inmate is indigent, the state will allow him to mail five first-class letters per week, at state expense. He will pay the state back if he receives money within a sixty-day period, but inmates who go sixty days without funds are not charged for indigent supplies.

Now I would like to move into the gray areas in prison commerce—gambling and extortion. And, for good measure, the black market.

Gambling is, of course, is prohibited, on the theory that it breeds violence. In reality, cases are rarely written for gambling, which is huge in prison. Inmates bet on games. They play parlays and boards—where you buy squares and win if you have the winning numbers, decided by the scores at the end of the time periods. Table games are constantly going on. Domino favorites are big six, knock, moon, forty-two, poker, and tonk. On some units, inmates make crude Monopoly games and play for real money. Inmates play Scrabble for a penny a point, which can get out of hand if you're playing twenty games a weekend and losing fifty points a game.

Hustlers abound. Inmates who don't get money draw up the parlays, run the boards, then sink the profits into tennis shoes or fans. They will then run raffles, say, for a championship fight. They will sell eleven chances for a bag of coffee per round—keeping one chance for themselves—and drag in eleven bags, or $18.40 for a fan that costs $12.00 when new. If the outcome of an event is in doubt, someone will lay a bet on it. So, a lot of money sent to inmates goes to pay their gambling debts. Many inmates are constantly in debt, are seen as marks, and have other inmates forever trying to make bets with them.

Now, let's talk about extortion. By this, people mean something taken through force; payment made from fear. In Texas prisons, there is a particularly ugly concept called "riding." If inmate A is riding with inmate B, then inmate A is paying inmate B with money or sex to take care of him, and for all intents and purposes inmate A is owned by inmate B. I have seen auctions where an inmate who was riding was sold for thirty or forty dollars, or for a pair of free-world tennis shoes.

Most inmates who ride do so out of fear, a few out of physical weariness after being beaten into submission. On many units, most young Anglo inmates will be tested, time and again, by Hispanic and Black inmates, who sometimes declare that *no* white inmates will survive on those units unless they are riding. There are cited cases wherein groups of inmates targeted one inmate and beat him whenever the opportunity provided itself, for days, until that inmate died, a victim of his courage and the cowardice of the attackers. This is a fairly new phenomenon in TDCJ. An inmate once had to fight a few times until he had demonstrated he had courage. Now the purpose is to break spirits. More on this in the chapter on Racism and Violence.

Officers know of the practice of riding and will periodically lock up the more vicious predators. However, most officers have contempt for inmates in general and for those in particular who they perceive as being weak and unable to "take care of their business," and they will not intervene unless some outside force compels them. Also, since it is generally known that at one time or another, and usually quite often, almost all Anglos on certain units will be called out to fight, many newcomers on those units simply agree to pay protection to veteran convicts. That is what riding is all about—trying to persuade convicts with money to pay in order to be left to do their time in peace. An inmate who is providing protection for an inmate who is riding is able to do so because he has enough respect built up that other inmates know he (or his gang) will retaliate if the protection is not honored. This is called "respecting the game," and is how riding survives—by the winking acquiescence of all involved, all inmates secretly glad *they* have not been forced to ride, and hoping the next frightened victim will land in *their* cell and will then pay *them* money.

Once an inmate catches a ride, he will be left alone. He may lose respect from other inmates, especially those who have fought and fought, but for some inmates, that is an acceptable trade-off; they pay so much per month and know they will do their time without being hassled. Once they do ride, however, eventually someone will expect them to provide sex, and if a man is willing to have sex with them, he will have had sex with many others in prison. This is why the incidence of AIDS in prison is many times that in the free-world. It is a contributing factor to the alarming rise of AIDS among the minority communities in Texas and the U.S.—members of their community go to prison, have homosexual sex, become infected, and then have sex with their wives or girlfriends.

If your relative is young, weak, and afraid, riding is an option he may well consider. This is a Texas prison reality. Officials will tell you that it doesn't exist, or that if it does, that the inmate need only ask for protection and it will be granted. That is not true, and I explain why in the chapter on Racism and Violence. Some inmates make peace with themselves and pay a certain amount each month. Most don't, and accept the certainty that they will face beating after beating.

This is one of the ugliest things about prison—we will take advantage of the weak and will turn eyes away from those being taken advantage of, believing that intervention will bring retaliation. If you think your relative or friend is riding, talk to him. Tell him you understand the pressures involved. Speaking with administration officials will likely do little, unless your relative or friend is willing to try to obtain safekeeping status, which is very difficult to do. Unless the more honorable and empathetic convicts decide to intervene and put a stop to this practice, it will continue to exist in Texas prisons.

And finally, the black market activities. TDCJ prohibits what it calls Trafficking and Trading. Specifically, this means that what I have was 1) issued to me, 2) bought by me, 3) mailed to me through official channels, or 4) brought in by me when I arrived. I am not allowed to give anything away. I am not allowed to accept anything from another inmate. He cannot buy me a soda. I cannot give him an envelope. I cannot loan him my radio. If I do these things, or if he does these things, we may receive disciplinary cases, and have the radio, soda, or envelope confiscated as contraband. However, like all else in prison, this is enforced selectively. Most officers will not say anything if they see me giving an inmate a cold soda when I return from the commissary, or if I give him a carton of soup. But if I bring a case of twenty-four soups out of my cell, then I am on my way to pay a debt or buy something, and most officers will confiscate the soups and give me a disciplinary case. Anything of value brought from the store—tennis shoes and the larger electrical items—are issued with property papers for the item, and the item itself is engraved with the purchaser's TDCJ number. By the rules, I am not allowed to sell any items or buy any items to or from other inmates. But if my money gets tight and I hit a losing streak on the domino table, I may want to sell my radio or fan. Someone will be willing to buy them, if for no other reason than to resell them.

Also, this being prison, items are stolen all the time and taken to different living quarters and sold. Usually, items are stolen only from people who have relatively little inluence, or because they have not earned the respect that would stop someone from stealing their property. In a winked-at agreement between officers and inmates, if somebody steals my property and I can prove that to an officer, he will very likely allow me to call that inmate out to fight until I am satisfied that my honor is intact. This is called "taking care of your business."

Cigarettes are a hot commodity in prison. Since they were declared illegal in March of 1995, their price has fluctuated, but one cigarette will cost from one to two dollars, usually "good money," which means food, not "junk money," or cosmetics. Drugs are harder to come by, but are available. More on this in an upcoming chapter.

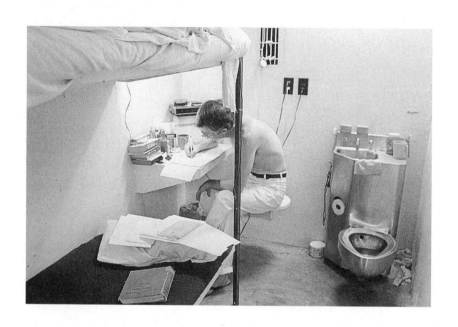

CHAPTER TEN

mail

*I*nmates in TDCJ are allowed to receive mail from anyone in the world, without any restrictions on amounts of First Class personal mail. The key word here is "personal." As long as there are no enclosures in mail to an inmate—no stamps, cash, pressed flowers, gold chains, etc.—the inmate will be given that letter. The actual, written content of the letter may be cause for denial, but I'll get to that in a minute.

The liberty allowed Texas inmates with their personal mail is not extended to packages. It is easier to say what inmates can receive than to list what they cannot.

Inmates can receive two types of packages:

1) Books or magazines, which must come from the publisher or bookstore. This means that you must order them from the publisher and have the publisher mail them directly to the inmate; or you must buy them at the bookstore yourself, give the bookstore the inmate's name, number, and address, and have the bookstore mail the books and magazines directly to the inmate. *Do not* try to mail books directly to the inmates. TDCJ mailrooms have a list of approved bookstores—if a package of books has a

made-up address and label, it will not appear on the approved list and will be rejected and returned.

I do not know if TDCJ will provide the list of approved bookstores to people requesting it. If you wish, call the agency in Appendix G that is listed as Offender Mail Service, which is in charge of inmate correspondence. However, from my understanding, any bookstore or publishing house that is legitimate and solvent need only contact TDCJ in order to be verified as such. In other words—if you buy books at a reputable store or order them from a reputable publishing company, TDCJ will accept the books. The content of the books may make them objectionable, but that is another matter.

2) Inmates may receive stationery, which includes legal pads, typing paper, ruled writing paper, and blank envelopes. The stationery must also come from an established bookstore, office supply, or similar shop, or it will be rejected. You can even order personalized stationery—matching paper and envelope from a company and have that mailed to an inmate—although that's a little too cute for most male inmates.

That's it. Don't even try anything else. You *can not* mail food, clothes, watches, photo albums, typewriters—no packages whatsoever. TDCJ makes no exceptions.

There are two items you can include with regular mail that will usually make it through with little hassle—photographs or clippings from newspapers. Use good sense. A photo of friends with their babies will not be a problem, but a friend obviously smoking a joint and flashing a hand sign may not be allowed in, and may subject the inmate to close scrutiny as a suspected gang member. Both incoming and outgoing mail is randomly read and scanned. About the only way an inmate will not be allowed to correspond with someone is if they discuss criminal activity, which is pretty stupid if you know your mail is being read.

Persons who receive mail from inmates and do not want those inmates to write them can notify the warden or other TDCJ official. The inmate will be ordered to not write that person, and his mail will be monitored. If he continues to write that person, he will be disciplined and be subject to criminal prosecution. Regular mail is mailed out un-sealed by inmates and sealed by mailroom employees after scanning or reading. Special mail—to government officials, lawyers, to the media, or to TDCJ officials—may be sealed by inmates. Incoming special mail is opened in the presence of the inmate and checked for physical contra-band but not read by the mailroom staff. Or at least, that is the set policy. There is no way for an inmate to prove if an employee has interfered with a particularly anticipated letter from or to an attorney or journalist.

I once wrote an article on gang-related violence for a Texas newspa-per doing a series on prison violence. When the article appeared, the entire series was sent to me by the newspaper as a courtesy. The package was clearly marked "Media mail," and I should have been called to the mailroom and the package opened in front of me. It was opened, read, denied, and *then* I was called to the mailroom and told so. Thus does the mailroom adhere to policy—when it is convenient.

The mail is distributed to the blocks at different times on different units. The individual guards working the blocks pass out the mail to inmates, either calling out names and cell locations, or making out a mail list, posting it, and having the inmate come by and ask for his mail. TDCJ promises to deliver all mail to inmates no later than forty-eight hours after it has been accepted by the mailroom, or in the case of long weekends, seventy-two hours. In my experience, this is mostly true.

Mail rules are relatively simple and are liberal for U.S. prisons. The only mail frowned upon and heavily censored—other than gang-related mail restrictions, which heavily penalize young Hispanics for their un-fortunate use of street slang and the mailroom censors' unfamiliarity with that slang—are pornographic books and magazines, and books and magazines that are about weapons, fighting, drug manufacturing, overt racial hatred, or related subjects.

You never really know if a magazine or book will be objected to, and what is allowed on one unit may be disallowed on another. The hardcore homosexual magazines will definitely be denied, as will be *Soldier of Fortune*. All else is subject to whoever runs a particular mailroom, and of course to the warden's likes and dislikes. For example, Stephen King's *Different Seasons* was taken off the shelves on Robertson Unit because it had a story of a prison escape, "The Shawshank Redemption." However, it was not removed from the shelves of the Wynne or Walls libraries. If a magazine or book is denied on the unit level, the inmate is notified and the magazine or book sent to Huntsville, where a decision is made by the Director's Review Committee to allow the publication in, to clip certain pages, or to deny it totally. This decision may not be appealed.

If an inmate is a suspected or confirmed gang member, his mail is closely scrutinized. If you write him in any sort of code, if your photos to him are of groups of young, partying friends, if TDCJ officials in any way believe that you are passing information of gang activities, they will reject that letter. This means they will call the inmate to the mailroom, give him a slip saying that they are not allowing this particular piece of mail in and then allow him to appeal the decision, which is rarely, if ever, overturned.

TDCJ has a policy resulting from the *Guajardo v. McAdams* decision, which I referred to in the chapter on Texas prison history. That case reformed the rules of correspondence for Texas inmates. Part of the policy states that if an inmate is denied a piece of mail, the following will be done: "[H]e will be either allowed to review the correspondence at the time of notification or he will be given a sufficiently detailed description of the rejected correspondence to permit effective utilization of the appeal procedure." (TDCJ-ID Correspondence Rules and Regulations Handbook.) This policy allows an inmate to base his appeal on a specific denial, and also allows him to tell whoever wrote the letter to please not do or say that specific thing again.

This policy is rarely followed. In reality, a denial will be vague, usually just a written notice saying the mail was denied because it was "gang-related." These determinations are usually made by unit gang intelligence officers, overwhelmingly Hispanic, who rely on their knowledge of Spanish and of the Hispanic culture to convince Anglo mailroom employees that letters written in Cholo—a mixture of English and Spanish slang—are all gang-related. In either case, a clear explanation of why a particular piece of mail has been denied is rarely given. So it is left to you, the letter writer, to understand that anything you write may be cause for that letter to be rejected, and for you to factor that in when you write an inmate.

It is impossible to overstate the importance of mail to an inmate. A large number of inmates never receive visits, or are visited rarely. Consistent and imaginative mail does wonders to combat the institutionalization process. By this I mean letters that do not come only on holidays. By this I mean postcards that are dropped in the mail on a normal day, with just a few words, to let an inmate know he is not forgotten, and that he is being written to not out of duty but from a sincere desire to communicate.

And by imaginative, I'll tell you what my wife does. She'll buy computer spreadsheets, those long rolls of perforated paper. She'll paint on them—colored eggs on Easter, or multicolored balls and trees for Christmas. She'll fold them and send them in a large manila envelope. When they arrive, I unwrap them and wind them all around my cell. Their color and festive design make me know, without a doubt, that someone cared enough to brighten my day, my drab cell—at least until some guard takes them down—with some time and attention. Use the mails to show your loved one a little attention. It may make a world of difference.

CHAPTER ELEVEN

visits and calls

*T*here are prisons in some states that allow conjugal visits between inmates and their spouses. There are prisons where visitors are encouraged to have picnics with their loved ones, who are allowed to bring in food, and the prisons provide barbecue facilities. Visits in those states are almost unsupervised, with inmates and their families left alone until they abuse the privilege. Texas is not one of those states. In Texas, it is assumed that all inmates will, if given the opportunity, smuggle in contraband or will otherwise abuse the visiting process. In order to prevent this, Texas limits the contact between visitors and convicts severely.

Visits in Texas prisons fall into two categories: general and special. General visits are further divided into two categories: contact and non-contact, or regular visits. Every convict in Texas prison is allowed some type of visit, unless he is in a locked-down status or in punitive segregation.

While an inmate is at Diagnostic, he is advised to designate ten people he would like to have on his visiting list. Each is subject to approval by TDCJ. Only ten adults are allowed on each inmate's list at any one time, and any adult not on that list will not be allowed to visit unless he or she applies with the unit warden and is approved for a special visit.

In general, inmates are allowed one two-hour visit, with two adults,

Saturday or Sunday, every weekend. The exceptions to this are: inmates still going through Diagnostic intake process, inmates in lockdown or some administrative segregation levels, and inmates in close custody, who are allowed either one or two visits per month. Visiting hours are from 8 A.M. to 5 P.M. Children under sixteen need not be on the visiting list and are not counted against the two-person limit. This means that a mother and aunt can visit, if both are on the list, and can bring a ten-year-old cousin, a five-year-old son, and a baby.

Regular visits are non-contact visits. These take place in one or two ways—either with the inmate and his family separated by and talking through a mesh screen, or separated by a glass partition and talking via telephones. Any adult on an inmate's approved visiting list will be allowed at least a regular visit, if the inmate meets all criteria. By this, I mean the inmate meets TDCJ-imposed criteria for visits—no disciplinary infractions that will deny visits, or things of that nature.

Contact visits are allowed only to immediate family, in most instances, unless special permission is granted by the warden. There are a few exceptions: in-laws, if accompanied by blood relatives; surrogate parents; and special relationships, if so approved by the warden. Only inmates in minimum custody, who are classified at least SAT IV (State Approved Trusty, see chapter twenty-one for a definition of all classifications), are allowed contact visits. Depending on a bewildering set of criteria, inmates who violate a wide range of unit policies may be denied contact visits. Cousins, fiancées, best friends, and others will not be allowed contact visits unless that inmate is assigned to an outside trusty camp, where all visits are contact.

During a contact visit, inmates are allowed to hug and kiss their adult visitors once when the visit begins and once when it ends. During the visit they will be allowed to hold hands with mothers and wives, from across the table. Only rarely will inmates be allowed to sit on the same side of a table with anyone other than a small child. If displays of affection become too provocative, and this varies from unit to unit and from officer to officer, the visit may be ended.

Visitors must have some sort of photo identification. They will be asked the name and TDCJ number of the inmate they are visiting, their relationship, and the visitor's current address. If the visitor is visibly drunk or high, he/she will not be allowed to visit. TDCJ has the right to ask to search visitors or their vehicles, and if refused, to deny the visit. All visitors will be asked to pass through a metal detector. Visitors are not allowed to bring photos, cameras, cigarettes, lighters, matches, books, magazines, or food. The only items allowed are a wallet, a clutch purse and a change purse. Beginning in late 2001, visitors were no longer allowed to bring in cash, but could bring change.

Visitors are encouraged to buy items from the vending machines located on some units for the inmates they are visiting. On other units they must hand the items to the guard on duty, who will pass them to the inmate. Some vending machines sell only cold drinks; some sell potato chips, candy, and other snacks. On some units, barbecue sandwiches or hamburgers will occasionally be sold to visitors and inmates. They must be consumed while visiting. Most units will allow photographs to be taken. These pictures will cost around three dollars, be taken by officers with instant cameras, paid for immediately by the visitors, and may be kept by inmates or their visitors.

All visitors must wear shirts and shoes. Halter-tops, sundresses, mesh skirts, fishnet shirts, or see-through shirts are not allowed. It is understandable that visitors want to look attractive. However, if they are dressed provocatively—especially females, in skirts with above-the-knee hemlines, low-cut tops or extremely tight pants—they will be asked to change or leave. This extends to younger females. My daughter was ten and was not allowed to visit because she was wearing a halter-top, and I saw an older woman, in her sixties refused because she was wearing culottes. If you are twenty miles from the nearest town, late on a Sunday afternoon, you may not have time to get other clothes. Don't jeopardize your visit. Dress conservatively and be safe. If your shirt has writing that can be considered vulgar or obscene, you may be denied a visit. Again, be smart.

Some inmates will ask their visitor to bring them money or drugs. This is incredibly stupid and selfish. If caught, visitors will 1) be immediately removed from the visiting room, 2) be removed from the inmate's visiting list 3) and very likely referred to local law enforcement agencies for prosecution. The inmate will also face punishment, which will include loss of good time, class and custody, and possible felony charges. It's just not worth it.

Inmates assigned to administrative segregation are allowed only regular visits, unless they are in protective custody, in which case they are allowed contact visits, in line with their disciplinary record.

Death Row Inmates are allowed regular (non-contact) visits only. In fact, inmates on Death Row are never again allowed to touch anyone in their family.

Special Visits

The warden may allow contact or non-contact visits outside of the normal visitation policy if you fall into the following categories:

1) If you must travel 300 miles or more, one-way, to visit. In this case, you may be allowed two special, four-hour visits, one on each weekend day. Contact the unit ahead of time to get approval. *Do not* just drive up, say you've come from Los Angeles, and expect to be granted a special, four-hour visit.

2) Spiritual advisor visits. If you identify yourself as a pastor, preacher, minister, or some recognized spiritual advisor, the warden may grant you a special visit even if you are not on the approved visitor's list.

3) Prospective employer visits. If you wish to employ an inmate and you present the proper identification, you will be allowed to visit that inmate. Contact the unit beforehand.

4) Media visit. If you are a member of the media, can present the proper credentials, and can show a need to interview an inmate, you may be allowed to visit an inmate.

5) If an inmate is seriously or critically ill, the warden may make special arrangements for him to have visits other than those normally allowed.

One last thing. *Please*, call on either Thursday or Friday before every visit. The unit may have gone on lockdown; your relative may be in solitary; he may have been transferred and the letter he wrote was late in arriving. Call the unit during working hours and ask if your relative is still there, if he is eligible for visits, and if you are still on the list. It takes a few minutes and a few dollars, but may save you a weekend and a few hundred dollars. Check the unit directory in the back of this book for the telephone numbers of all units.

Telephone Calls

TDCJ does not have pay phones on any of its units and will not have them in the near future. Anything you have been told to the contrary is simply not true.

It is TDCJ policy to allow eligible inmates "reasonable access" to telephones. At the risk of belaboring the point, every warden will define reasonable in a different fashion, although TDCJ written policy suggests once every ninety days. It is *not* policy to accept incoming calls or messages, unless there is a verifiable emergency involved.

To be allowed a call, an inmate must have had a clear disciplinary record for at least ninety days; must be working or in school; and must submit a phone call request to the official responsible for granting phone calls on his unit—usually the unit building major. If approved, the inmate will be called to the area designated for telephone calls as close as possible to the time of the day which he has requested, although many units simply schedule all calls between 6 and 9 P.M. The inmate will give the guard the number to be called. Inmates are only allowed to call those individuals on their approved visiting list. The call must be collect. The inmate will usually be allowed to try an additional number if the desired party is not at home.

Each unit may place different lengths on calls by inmates, although TDCJ policy ostensibly limits calls to five minutes and to three during high-volume times such as Thanksgiving or Christmas. Calls are monitored, and loud, boisterous conversations are not allowed. If an inmate threatens anyone, uses obscene language, asks for money or exhibits what is considered abusive behavior while on the telephone, the call will be terminated.

Inmates are allowed to receive phone calls from their attorney. A request for an attorney-inmate phone call must be made by the attorney. He or she should call the unit warden, explaining his or her desire to speak with the inmate. In most cases, this request will be honored, especially if the date looms for a court appearance or hearing and time and distance make a visit difficult for the attorney. The call will be scheduled between 8 A.M. and 5 P.M., unless the attorney presents a compelling need for another time. The call will not be monitored and its duration will not be set but will depend on the topic and seriousness of the situation. If social or non legal matters are being discussed, the call will be terminated.

CHAPTER TWELVE

religion

*I*f adversity draws one closer to the Lord, the skies over most prisons should be ringing with hymns and the fences humming with prayer. Most convicts were not religious people before coming to jail—that truth is evident in their reckless, hurtful, selfish actions. However, the Lord is active in Texas prisons. Inmates who wish to pursue a spiritual awakening are extended almost every opportunity to do so. TDCJ extends quite a bit of freedom to inmates for them to pursue individual beliefs and practices. All inmates are encouraged to believe, worship, and to study their particular religion. Participation in any worship is voluntary, unless an inmate is assigned to one of the pre-release units that has a focus on spiritual fellowship as a foundation for rehabilitation, such as the Carol Vance Unit, which houses the Inner Change Faith-Based Treatment Program.

Many things contribute to the degree of religious freedom and array of religious activities on a particular unit: the dedication of the unit chaplains; the involvement of community volunteers; the religious beliefs of the warden. In any case, this is one area where what TDCJ practices often exceed what its policy requires.

When an inmate arrives at Diagnostic, he designates any religious preference. In order to change affiliations, he must notify Unit Classification of his desire to do so. He may do this by mailing a letter to Classification, or by asking the unit chaplain for assistance, but he must notify someone of his intent to change his religious preference, and he can only change once a year. This is important. For example, if an inmate says at Diagnostic that he is Baptist and later becomes involved in Islam, he will not be recognized as such unless he notifies Classification. He will not be allowed to purchase or keep a prayer rug or be served a meal consistent with Islamic practices, unless he officially changes religion. He may read the Quran and go to Islamic services and order Islamic literature, of course, but if a recognized group receives particular benefits, an inmate must officially say he is part of that group to receive those benefits.

While inmates may practice a particular religion, they will not be given meeting space unless they are part of a group. A group—whether of Buddhists, Baptists, or Jehovah Witnesses—must include at least fifteen inmates on a particular unit. At that point, if recognized by the warden, the group will be granted meeting space on a pro rata basis. The time and space allowed will be dependent on the percentage of the unit population that the requesting faith group represents. This is why Catholic and Protestant services get the most time and space. Chaplains are available on every unit, and some units have volunteer chaplains in addition to the one or two that are employed by the state. Chaplains are responsible for developing and conducting the programs of worship and often will invite and encourage local volunteers to enter the prison to minister to inmates.

If you are interested in spreading your faith at a prison near you, contact the chaplain's office at the prison and ask to meet with him or her. TDCJ has a set of criteria that volunteers must meet, but that criteria may change from month to month, and the training expected of volunteers may also change. It is not so easy as just walking through the prison gates. Because the standards are so dictated by the warden's wishes, I will not attempt to describe the criteria any particular person needs to meet before being allowed to enter the prison to minister to inmates.

Periodically, various faith and gospel groups will drop in on Texas prisons for a weekend or weeklong revival. The Bill Glass Crusade, Chaplain Ray ministries, and the Kenneth Copeland ministry (featuring ex-Houston Oiler Mike Barber,) are some of the religious groups that have seen fit to bless Texas inmates with regular visits. There are also local gospel groups that may come onto a particular unit on religious holidays to accompany a unit choir in hymnal celebration and to share their testimony. There is a Kairos program offered on many units, which consists of local religious volunteers who form mentor relationships with inmates who desire a closer relationship with an older person who may help them in their religious studies. Contact the chaplain at your local prison if you are interested in mentoring an inmate.

The chapels on the different units vary enormously in size and character. On Wynne, there is a huge, ornate chapel, with conventional pews and seating for hundreds. On the newer units, the chapel may be a room with a slightly raised dais, with folding chairs that may seat fifty cramped inmates and visitors. Inmates often form informal prayer and Bible study groups, and it is these spontaneous sessions that form the foundation of most religious activities in prison. These groups are formed from a deep desire to strengthen those inmate's spiritual values, and their informal structure and setting lends them a strength and validity that many formal meetings lack. The unit wardens often give these informal groups time and space for mini-revivals.

Inmates may receive and keep scriptural and devotional books and religious periodicals, so long as they are mailed via proper channels, from bookstores, publishers, or through the chaplain's offices. Pastoral visits are afforded on every unit. Pastors, ministers, priests, rabbis, monks, nuns, imams, etc., are permitted to visit inmates on ministerial/spiritual matters. Each inmate is allowed two such visits per month, provided his spiritual advisor presents credentials and makes arrangements at least twenty-four hours in advance.

Inmates in the following groups are allowed the mentioned religious articles. Contact the warden or the chaplain at the unit if you want to send any of these religious items to an inmate.

> Catholics—cross or crucifix, religious medal, rosary.
> Jews—yarmulkah, tallis.
> Muslims—prayer rug, koofi, prayer beads.
> Sikh—turban, wood comb.
> Native American—headband, shell, medicine bag, sacred stones, feather. Drums, pipe, tobacco, gourd, sage, sweetgrass, and cedar are allowed but must be stored with the chaplain for ceremonial use.

The above list may not be all-inclusive. Ask the chaplain for details if your friend or relative is interested in a particular religion/group and you are willing to help.

CHAPTER THIRTEEN

general and law libraries

*A*ll TDCJ units provide inmates access to both a general library and to a legal library. However, access to the general library is considered a privilege that can be revoked for disciplinary infractions. On the other hand, every inmate in TDCJ—whether in solitary confinement, in the lowest levels of administrative segregation, or in transit—will be able to either visit the legal, or law, library or have legal materials brought to him. The courts have held that TDCJ cannot deny any meaningful access to the courts, and the system, in my opinion, has done a decent job of fulfilling that mandate.

While access to the legal libraries is pretty uniform throughout the system, there is a wide gap between what access is allowed by the different units to their general libraries. The libraries are attached to the unit educational departments and are usually supervised by librarians with free-world training and staffed by TDCJ officers with a few convict clerks to perform the checking in and out of books, updating card catalogues, etc. Access to the library itself is dictated by security. As security on the different units is dictated by the attitude of the wardens and higher-ranking officers, one unit may be more accommodating of inmates who desire to use the library, while others may consider it an unnecessary privilege and a security headache. So, one unit may offer each inmate two hours weekly in the library, while another may leave the library open all evening to any inmate who is otherwise unoccupied. One unit may call inmates from separate living quarters on a sporadic basis, or only call thirty inmates at a time, and then allow them to stay only fifteen minutes at a time, hardly enough time to browse, much less read a newspaper or magazine.

Most units have the current issues of national magazines, including *Time, Newsweek, Ebony, Jet, Cycle World, Hot Rod, Discover, Rolling Stone, Christina, Black Beat, National Enquirer, National Geographic, ESPN Magazine, Popular Mechanics, Hispanic, Sporting News, and TV Guide.* Most libraries will also have subscriptions to the larger Texas metropolitan daily newspapers, along with *USA Today* and some smaller, local papers.

However, unless an inmate is in school and thus goes to the library with his class on a weekly basis for two hours at a time, or lives on a unit with liberal library privileges, he will rarely get more than a few moments to glance at a magazine. They are not for checkout purposes, and anyone caught taking one or ripping out pages will receive a case. Neither will he be allowed to keep old magazines. The volume of magazines is tremendous, and it would be easy for units to give old issues of magazines away, but the popular ones find their way to the officers' barbershop, while the rest are simply tossed out.

Inmates not on recreation restriction are allowed to check out books, usually on a weekly basis. Some units allow inmates to check out one book, some allow two. TDCJ dictates that its units have at least five books for each inmate, so a typical 2,500-man unit will have over 12,000 books. The books will cover a spectrum—non-fiction, how-to-books, language, Spanish-language, career, history, religion, psychology, and of course fiction: from Lynn Abbey to Roger Zelazny, and many authors in between. TDCJ cannot be faulted for its library resources.

But, and it bears repeating—access to the library is so sporadic that on many units only a handful of inmates, other than those allowed to take Windham classes, get meaningful access to any given library. This means that if an inmate is in college and wants to do in-depth research, he will most likely need someone in the free-world to assist him in obtaining reference materials, because he will not have the chance or the time to use the ones in the unit library.

Before *Ruiz v. Estelle,* Texas prisons had abysmal records when it came to allowing inmates time and opportunity to do legal research or fight their convictions in a meaningful way. In fact, inmates who insisted on doing legal work—writ writers, as they were and are called—were frequently beaten by guards and by "building tenders". "Building tender" is the generic term for inmates who were used by prison officials to perform certain supervisory duties. This was common in the South—many Southern prisons made it a practice to put prisoners in charge of other prisoners. Louisiana armed its inmate flunkies, as did Arkansas, and a judge's comments marveling at the criteria Arkansas used to select its inmate guards hinted at the type of men that building tenders were: "Actually, few, if any objective criteria are used in selecting trusties; that a man is a bad man, or a dangerous man, or that he has a bad criminal record is by no means a disqualification; on the contrary, it may be a recommendation." *Holt v. Sarver II*, 412 F.2d 304 (8th Cir. 1971.) More on this in chapter twenty.

But *Ruiz* changed all that. Every TDCJ unit has either a law library or a mini-library, depending on the unit's purpose. The regular ID units will have the fully stocked libraries, while the transfer facilities and state jails will mostly have the smaller libraries that depend on loaning programs to fill the gaps.

Inmates are allowed a minimum of ten hours per week in the law library. They usually request time, and if they are in at least medium custody, will then be given a pass to the library during a time that does not interfere with their work hours. Inmates in close custody or ad/seg are not allowed to visit the law library. For those inmates, unit law libraries will either deliver copies of requested cases or allow them to request delivery of specific law books and reference materials. Law library clerks will deliver those materials, and in twenty-four to forty-eight hours, pick them up along with new requests for other materials. TDCJ currently allows those inmates to request three separate references three times per week, down from five references five times per week just a few years ago.

If inmates desire, they can request legal visits with other inmates of like custody. This means that if I am working on an appeal, and if inmate

Jonesy in Building Four has a similar case and has already filed his appeal, I may want to discuss things with him. The unit law library supervisor will allow both of us to meet in the unit law library for up to two hours at a time, three or four days a week, until we abuse the privilege. Unfortunately, there are inmates who use this opportunity to set up gang meetings, to pass contraband, or just to visit. But most visits in the law library are between convicts who are sincerely attempting to learn the legal ropes, enough to fight a possible case of prosecutorial misconduct. The unit law libraries also provide notary services to inmates who request them.

CHAPTER FOURTEEN

craft shop

*T*here are perhaps only three ways an inmate may legally make money while he is in TDCJ. One is to write and then market his fiction, essays and poetry to free-world magazines. Another is to paint or draw and sell his artwork to interested buyers outside the walls. Both of these moneymaking ideas are subject to not just individual talent but to the mails, and to the hit-and-miss assistance of outside parties.

TDCJ offers one way for inmates who keep clear disciplinary records to make money while inside the walls, with all work and most sales being done by the inmates. It's called the craft shop, or the "piddling" shop, and it is a privilege not to be dismissed lightly. The craft shop is just that: an area where inmates work on leather goods, jewelry, wood projects, paintings, fanciful stick creations—any of a number of personal expressions that can be done at a minimum of cost and then sold to officers or visitors or marketed to the free-world.

Inmates within the shops, called piddlers, usually begin as apprentices, or helpers, and work their way up the ladder as space in the craft shop allows. A determined, hard-working piddler who produces quality goods can make over $12,000 a year while still performing his assigned duties for the system. That may not sound like much money, but it does wonders for the inmate. He supports himself. He is not a drain on his family's financial resources. He is able to send goods—purses, rings, jewelry boxes—and even money home to his family. Most importantly, his return to the free-world is not as frightening because he leaves TDCJ with money for the basic necessities, usually enough to cushion him for the first few months, and he has developed a marketable skill he can rely on in his search for employment.

The craft shop is open to all inmates, but a spot in it is a privilege. To apply for a piddling card, inmates must be assigned to a job, have been in the system for at least six months, and they must be at least minimum custody. Piddling cards are assigned on a first-come, first-served basis, at least in theory. If you fit the criteria, you go on the list. If a piddler leaves, a helper moves up the ladder and the helper's slot is filled by an inmate on the waiting list.

Although it may not seem fair to those without funds, an inmate must keep a certain balance on his books in order to be allowed to apply for a piddling card. Depending on the craft the inmate will pursue, this amount will be from $25 to $100. Any inmate applying for a card who does not maintain that balance will not be considered for a card. This is because TDCJ provides nothing but the work area, the craft shop itself. It has tables, electrical outlets, and lockers for storage. If I want to work leather, and I finally get my piddling card and am admitted to the shop, I have nothing—no tools, no leather, no contracts, and no way to begin. I must have a lump sum of money to order the basic necessities of my craft.

A few inmates may have the money to order tools and leather right away, but most don't. Most start with very little. They begin as helpers and apprentice themselves to experienced piddlers, who will allow them to use tools and give them scraps of leather in exchange for assistance. Apprentices cut leather and lace together cut pieces, the dreaded drudgery of leather working. As they learn the ropes, apprentices get a small percentage of the projects they assist on. They also use the scraps to make small projects of their own. They begin to order materials for their own use and begin to make larger, more expensive goods. Some piddlers make boots, saddles, and chaps from scratch for exacting field officers or for officers who are working cowboys or rodeo participants. The better the apprentice and the more work he produces, the more equipment he has and the more work he can then produce. The cycle feeds itself. Some piddlers have thousands of dollars in equipment and supplies, five or six helpers and spend every available moment aside from their assigned jobs in the craft shop.

The system is the same for all crafts, except maybe art, a more solitary pursuit. TDCJ understands how important a piddling card is to inmates, and the waiting list may be hundreds of names long. So, to gauge inmates' sincerity, TDCJ requires those waiting to keep a minimum balance, and those with cards to order a certain amount of supplies each quarter, evidence that they are producing crafts and not just taking up space.

Piddlers sell their goods through three methods—direct sales to visitors or unit employees; contract sales to visitors or unit employees; or by sending goods outside to be marketed by family or friends. Some units have display areas—usually a spot that visitors to a unit will be sure to pass—and will allow piddlers to place a few items there. Visitors may buy what is on display by filling out the required paperwork and depositing a check or money order in the piddler's account. Or visitors may request an item be made for them by a particular piddler by doing what TDCJ employees must do—filling out a work order or a contract.

Officially, if an employee wants a piece from the craft shop, he or she is required to contact the craft shop supervisor, who will then assign the job to the inmate best equipped to fill the order. In reality, employees approach inmates, especially those who already have done work for them or other employees, discuss what they want and fill out a contract specifying what will be done for what price. Employees are allowed to provide materials for special contracts. For example, if an officer wants a leather purse for his daughter and wants inmate Smith to make it, the officer will ask the inmate how much material he needs. The officer will buy the leather, bring it to the inmate, and contract only for the labor.

The third marketing method, and by far the most lucrative, is to have an outlet in the free-world. As long as inmates keep their status and class in TDCJ and fulfill all craft shop and unit requirements, they may make as many items as time and material permit and send them out. Some inmates have family members sell their pieces at craft fairs or in small boutiques. Others contract directly with stores and work on percentages.

Some have websites set up. Some units allow inmate-to-inmate contracts, with the goods being sent to the buying inmate's family, and the buying inmate signing a contract agreeing to have the purchase price deducted from his account. However it is done, having a free-world outlet is every piddler's goal.

Prices are set by the piddlers themselves and are adjusted according to how quickly a craft item sells. In any given craft shop, numerous inmates will make comparable items, all priced similarly. As in the free-world, attention to quality and a willingness to customize soon garners a craftsman a steady stream of customers.

As in everything in TDCJ, there is a tremendous difference between craft shops on different units. Some encourage piddling and provide large shops and generous piddling time and offer display areas. (By "generous piddling time," I mean that those units call the inmates to the craft shop at all times of the day. It is not so easy as just walking out of the cell and down to the craft shop. One must wait for the craft shop supervisor to arrive, to open the shop, to call the inmates. Some units assign an employee permanently to the craft shop; others make it a revolving assignment. As can be expected, the permanent supervisors are more responsible.)

Some units are much more restrictive and set difficult standards, with craft shops populated by the warden's favored inmates. Some units allow in-cell piddling cards, which are low-cost cards for inmates who draw with colored pencils, paint with water colors, or create small items from toothpicks or matchsticks.

Many piddlers use the craft shop as a way of improving their quality of life while in prison. They make just enough money to buy food, to gamble, and to occasionally mail something home. However, a diligent piddler will have no problem clearing $1,000 a month with an outside outlet. A few inmates, especially those in jewelry and woodcrafts, may make over $30,000 a year, after taxes. I've known piddlers who put their children through college while in prison. But for most piddlers, the craft shop is a way to improve their prison existence and to soften their landing when they are finally released.

CHAPTER FIFTEEN

substance abuse

*T*his will be a short chapter. The inescapable truth is that there exists no meaningful substance abuse treatment program for the great majority of Texas convicts. Regrettably, this seems to be the direct result of public opinion. In 1990, newly elected Governor Ann Richards promised a new era in the way Texas would approach its exploding prison population. Recognizing that much of crime in Texas was committed by men and women either under the influence of drugs or alcohol, or stealing to amass the money to buy drugs or alcohol, Richards proposed setting aside tens of thousands of prison beds to house substance abusers.

There would be entire units devoted to rehabilitating addicts—therapeutic communities where perimeter security would be enhanced by convict serenity; where counselors would attempt the radical notion of fighting crime by preventing it, instilling hope and self-esteem into addicts who until then had known only the dreary treadmill of jail, dope, and crime.

Governor Richards was promptly voted out of office and the new governor, George W. Bush, ensured that those units were instead given over to housing parole violators, drunk drivers, and the occasional violent criminal. The state is committed to eradicating crime by having enough

beds for anyone who commits a crime, not by addressing such subjective and intangible concepts as poverty, despair, and rehabilitation. Therefore, its substance abuse program is the bare minimum necessary to
demonstrate to the occasional liberal legislator or convict-friendly group
that TDCJ does, indeed, offer such a program.

The prison system has a three-pronged program for inmates, and all
three prongs are reserved for convicts whose parole is imminent. The
first, grandly titled the Institutional Division Substance Abuse Program,
consists of a twenty-four-hour substance abuse education program. Not
an around-the-clock, intensive program; a *total* of twenty-four hours,
during which a long-term addict is supposed to absorb enough information to combat his addiction. To be allowed into this particular program,
a convict's name must be submitted to the unit counselors by the parole
board, meaning the inmate is being considered for parole.

Participation in the two other programs—the In-Unit Prison Therapeutic Community, lasting nine to twelve months, and the Pre-Release
Substance Abuse Program, a four-month course—must be approved by
the parole board, which essentially means an inmate has been approved
for release upon completion of the given course. The brutal fact is that,
according to one unit substance abuse counselor, the four-month program is "essentially useless," leaving the longer course, with parole-
supervised aftercare, as the only substance abuse program worthy of its
name.

So, for the 120,000 inmates in TDCJ's thirty-nine maximum and
medium security units and its five transfer facilities who are not eligible
for parole at any given time, the only care offered is self-help groups.
Quoting from a 1997 pamphlet entitled "Substance Abuse Treatment
Programs," "Self-help groups, such as Alcoholics Anonymous, (AA) and
Narcotics Anonymous, (NA) and SOS (Secular Organization for Sobri-
ety) are available, and participation is voluntary."

In plain English: TDCJ will not offer an inmate any sort of structured
program to help him combat his addiction *until he is considered eligible
for release*. If he has a twenty-year aggravated sentence for a robbery
committed while under the influence of cocaine, and if that crime was
the latest in a long line of drug-influenced crimes, that inmate will do
the time necessary to become eligible for parole without any meaningful

attempt by the system to address that addiction, until the parole board is considering him for parole. At that time, he will be given a week's worth of classes, and if approved for release, will be shunted into a program that is supposed to address a problem the system ignored up until then.

There occasionally arises an isolated effort to nourish inmates' attempts to change. Both the Estelle and Wynne units, and perhaps others, recently had set aside living areas for convicts who agreed to give up some autonomy and live in a group-oriented setting, centered around twelve-step principles. The wardens on those particular units are to be commended for making an effort to provide an atmosphere conducive to change, meager as those efforts seem to some. However, those groups are hampered by a lack of counselors—each having at most two counselors trained in substance abuse recovery—and minimal literature/video resources. As a result, the focus of each group is usually determined by the convicts themselves, and they often fall prey to petty politics and prison games.

The cold truth is that TDCJ's decision to stress punishment over drug rehabilitation reflects the public's perception that drug rehab programs are a waste of time and money. The only way that will change is through a concerted lobbying effort from citizen groups. The recent success of Proposition 36 in California, which created a huge substance abuse infrastructure for many newly decriminalized or downgraded felony acts, shows that there is a growing recognition that mere possession of drugs cannot and should not be addressed by simply throwing people into prison for years on end. There is a sense around the country that the Drug War cannot be won, and that its casualties are not only the men and women who are incarcerated, but their families and the tremendous outlays of public funds going into the costs of incarceration, funds better spent on true substance abuse programs.

But those sentiments have not taken a foothold in Texas, except perhaps in isolated county jails, where an enlightened sheriff takes the initiative to insist on substance abuse programs in his jail. Such is the case in Travis County, where the district attorney has for years set the standard for such programming.

Having said all that, it is possible for a convict to overcome his addiction while in TDCJ. He must do it on his own, however, by attending NA and AA, and by relying on the assistance of volunteers and fellow convict addicts. On almost every unit, the convict population has formed a combined NA/AA group that is supported by local, free-world groups—many of them comprised of former convicts—which send in volunteers to share their experiences and offer support and literature. Most units call NA meetings at set times throughout the week, and each meeting will last an hour or so.

Most meetings are reserved for minimum custody inmates, and they are not allowed to take off time from their jobs to attend meetings. The correctional staff on some units foster an atmosphere of contempt for inmates who attend NA/AA meetings, announcing a meeting by saying, "Wino Call!" or some such stupidity. On those units, the guards working the desks—whose job it is to inform the officers working the cell blocks that a meeting has been called—will often not do so, or call the inmates out late, or do what they can to hinder a convict's participation in those meetings.

But all of those things can be dealt with by an inmate who is sincere in seeking recovery. In fact, those barriers can be turned to his advantage, if he can share with his group at large how he has learned to accept the behavior of those over which he has no control, and the growth that signifies. If your convict friend or relative has an addiction, you should encourage him to attend NA/AA meetings, and you may want to seek out local Al/Anon groups, which are comprised of non-addict relatives and friends of addicts. You will meet people who have experienced the same heartbreak you have, and perhaps you can exchange and share methods of dealing with the problems caused by your incarcerated loved ones, along with ways to help them.

education

*I*f there is only one thing you can do to assist your convict friend or relative in his struggle to prepare for freedom and remain out of prison, that one thing should be to encourage him to get an education. You may believe that his lack of spiritual values, or his addiction, led to his criminal actions, and you want him to attend AA/NA and get involved in religious programs. This is good because he needs to address those issues also. However, he can't read the Bible if he can't plain *read*. He can't complete the written portion of the Substance Abuse Treatment Program if he can't *write*. He won't be able to hold down a job, or be involved in the life of his family or the larger society, if he doesn't grasp the fundamental concepts that you take for granted—balancing a checkbook, following written directions, taking the state driver's license test, or forming a simple budget. He will have no connection with his neighbor or society if he knows nothing of the basic milestones of our history or doesn't understand the civic process.

Study after study of offenders, and the reasons they return or don't, has shown that the single biggest variable that can be controlled by convicts themselves is education. It's simple—the more education inmates get, the lower their rate of return to prison. Sure, there are men in prison with college degrees. But they are vastly outnumbered by the tens of thousands of men who dropped out in the eighth or ninth grades, turned to drugs and crime, went to prison, have never held a job, have never learned the rudiments of adult life. If those men don't acquire at least a basic education, they will never stand a chance in the free-world.

The good news is that a convict in Texas who wants to educate himself has a variety of programs to choose from—basic educational courses, vocational courses, and two-year, four-year, and graduate level college courses. The not-so-good news is that many of these courses are offered only on certain units. To qualify for transfer to those units, convicts must meet certain criteria—good time, class and status requirements—that can be readily taken away by unit disciplinary and classification committees, necessitating extremely good behavior from sometimes not-so-patient convicts.

Windham School District

The Windham School District (WSD), created by the Texas Legislature to serve only Texas prisons, has a school on almost every unit in Texas. (Some transfer facilities, trusty camps, or state jails may not.) In 1998-99, WSD had a seventy-seven million dollar budget and provided educational services to 74,441 inmates – 56,096 institutional division inmates and 18,345 state jail inmates. The primary purpose of WSD is to prepare students to successfully take the General Equivalency Diploma (GED) examination and earn their GEDs. In 1999, GEDs were awarded to 5,400 students.

Inmates whose Educational Achievement (EA) is less than 6.0 (of a 12.9) are automatically enrolled in WSD academic classes, and will continue to attend until they raise their EA scores to 6.0, attain a GED, or are removed for disciplinary reasons. Close custody and administrative segregation inmates are not allowed to take any type of classes, other than correspondence courses, if the warden approves. Most don't. Inmates with EA scores higher than 6.0, who are at least Line Class I and medium custody, may attend WSD if there is available room. Inmates with GEDs or high school diplomas are not allowed to take WSD classes other than college prep courses.

Students in WSD are grouped according to EA scores. The remedial, or special education classes, are for students who are basically illiterate and lack the fundamentals in almost every area of lower education. Once their scores are considered high enough, they will be funneled into classes that demand more of them. Windham is like any other school district in that it is always short of materials and its students are at the mercy of the initiative and energy shown by the individual principals and teachers. Like any district, WSD has terrible teachers and great teachers. The security orientation of prison further hampers WSD. The materials are rationed to inmates, as it is assumed that excess paper and pencils will be stolen by inmates. Because books are shared by different classes and thus precious, most WSD teachers—or rather, the security officers assigned to the school—prohibit students from taking books, study guides, or workbooks to their living quarters. However, some units may allow students who have shown respect for school materials and a desire to work outside of class to check out selected books.

Of course, WSD has no field trips. There is little laboratory work, and bilingual education is spotty. Every unit will have a computer lab for use by its WSD academic classes, but the programs are simple, and there is absolutely no access to the Internet. Most students attend classes three or four hours daily, five days a week, although some special education students may attend all day. Teachers have no individual areas of instruction—no biology, civics, or English teachers. Each teacher will teach many subjects to his or her class, and each class will have only one teacher. Learning is self-paced. While a teacher may give a general test over something all students studied in class, each student's overall progress is dictated by the improvement in his EA scores. EA testing is held on regularly scheduled days throughout the year, and if a student wants to take the test and is recommended by his teacher, he may, and if his scores have risen to a certain level, then be scheduled to take the GED test. Some students may take a decade to attain their GED, slowly working their way up the ladder, and some may ace the GED test on the first time and leave WSD right away.

Students who graduate are not always required to leave school. Each principal will have his or her own policy, and often, if a student is quiet, courteous, shows a desire to continue to learn, and is willing to assist the teacher in instructing other students, he may be allowed to stay enrolled in school.

WSD does everything possible to make students feel good about their accomplishments, recognizing that their previous failures may have contributed heavily to their lack of self-esteem and to their criminal problems. Each unit will hold graduation ceremonies for those students who have earned their GEDs during the previous period, and family will be allowed a special contact visit with graduating inmates at that time.

Vocational Courses

There are two types of vocational courses offered to Texas inmates— those offered by WSD, called Career and Technical Education (CTE), and those offered by various two-year colleges, for which those colleges will award credit toward a two-year degree. Windham offers thirty-seven courses in its CTE, including Diesel and Auto Mechanics; Small Engine Repair; Welding; Bricklaying; Barbering; Horticulture; Radio and TV Repair; Air Conditioning Repair; Data Entry; Truck Driving; and many more. (See the Unit Profiles appendix for a list of which courses are offered on what units.)

Although the statistics for the two-year college offerings were not available, WSD in 1999 had 15,285 institutional division inmates enrolled in CTE courses, along with 2,774 state jail inmates. During that year, WSD awarded 9,600 certificates on completion of CTE courses. Many, if not most, of the courses taught in prison were initially offered in order to train inmates to perform functions necessary to run the prison system itself. For example, the welding and diesel mechanic graduates were given jobs in the various transportation and maintenance departments; the graduates of the Culinary Skills course were assigned to the Officers' Dining Room; the barbering school grads cut hair. While the intent and motivation behind prison education now likely stems more from a public recognition that inmates need to learn useful skills in order to not turn immediately back to crime, many of the graduates still are given prison jobs that take advantage of their recent vocational course learning. Personally, I believe the on-the-job training is invaluable.

Policy is to limit each convict to two courses, but that isn't set in stone. A convict with a high school diploma, until recently, was not allowed to take a WSD vocational course, but that has changed. If there is room on the waiting list, an inmate with a high school diploma will be placed on the list and allowed to enroll in a CTE course. An inmate who gets his GED in prison may take two WSD courses and then later take college vocational courses also. Also, if an inmate targets courses of like subjects—small engine repair, auto mechanics and diesel mechanics—he may be allowed to take all three, if the waiting list permits. Entry into the courses is governed by a variety of criteria, including:

1) EA scores, which differ, some courses requiring at least an 8.0, others asking for a 6.5
2) Disciplinary record—inmates must be at least Line Class I, and in the case of Truck Driving School, be at least SAT II; and not have had a major case for at least six months, often a year
3) Approval by the state classification committee if the course is not offered on the unit an inmate is currently assigned to and he must transfer to another
4) Time left on his sentence—those closest to parole eligibility or discharge get first choice, if they fit all other criteria
5) Payment—students must pay for or promise to pay for all college vocational courses

Some courses are quite long—six to eight months, or 600 hours, and some are considered "short" courses, lasting 45 to 200 hours. All are taught by instructors who have not only demonstrated a proficiency in the subject matter but who have also passed certain training programs designed to hone their particular talents and keep them current. Depending on the subject matter, the equipment used will either be current or sadly dated. It is easier, and cheaper, to buy clippers for the barbers than it is to buy the computer-enhanced equipment used by mechanics. As a result, the classes sometimes avail themselves of equipment donated by free-world companies who are interested in supplying TDCJ in other areas, or are in the habit of hiring ex-convicts and desire that they have a good vocational foundation.

Upon completion of the particular courses, inmates are awarded certificates, and depending on the class, are certified by the relevant governmental body. The CTE courses are, by most accounts, just as difficult as the college vocational courses, which are six months long and result in not only a certificate of completion but also in twenty hours of college credit. The college courses are offered in nineteen areas, many of them in areas also offered by WSD. While the college courses may use more elevated language and be a bit more conceptual, all the trades are taught as thoroughly as possible, given the time and materials provided and, of course, the ability and motivation of the instructors and the diligence and willingness to learn of the inmates/students.

College

It remains to be seen how much longer higher education will be offered in Texas prisons. There is a belief, slowly spreading across the country, that any education other than the most basic is a waste of money that would be better spent building more prison cells or funding victim compensation programs. While Texas prison policy is punitive in nature and often dictated by extremely short-sighted administrators, the availability of higher education in Texas has been excellent in comparison to other, supposedly more enlightened states—such as Massachusetts, which no longer offers college courses to its prisoners.

For years, Texas convicts could take one college course free, paid for by the state. In addition, most were eligible for federal Pell grants that enabled them to take as many courses as they could handle without failing while still working at their prison job. Those days are over. Texas no longer pays for college courses, and the Pell grant is no longer available to convicts. Texas will allow eligible inmates to take one course per semester without immediately paying, but they must sign an agreement that they will reimburse the state upon release or face revocation of parole. Any additional courses the inmate desires must be immediately paid for.

There are exceptions to this, primarily those granted to veterans. Texas veterans with at least a general discharge under honorable conditions may attend college free of charge, via the Hazlewood Act, which pays the college tuition and fees of Texas veterans whose G.I. Bill benefits have expired. A veteran interested in availing himself of this opportunity should write the college counselor at his unit. He should also write the Veterans' Affairs Office, either in Washington, D.C., or in Houston, requesting a copy of his DD form 214, signifying his date and conditions of discharge, or other verification of his service.

Regardless of how an inmate pays for his college, he must first present evidence of his graduation from high school or evidence of a GED, and he then must pass whatever tests the state mandates from all its other graduates—the TAAS or TASP, or whatever is currently required. Any inmate coming into the system who wants to attend college should write his high school for a copy of his transcript and his diploma, or to the college he attended for the same. He should then contact the Continuing Education office at his unit, asking for the requirements to attend college. Most units don't offer college, and an inmate must meet the same requirements as those for an inmate requesting a transfer in order to take a vocational course.

If an inmate is allowed to transfer to a unit that offers college courses, as long as he is attending college, passing, and staying out of trouble, he will be allowed to stay at that unit until he graduates. If he wishes to pursue a four-year degree, he will then be transferred to one of the units offering that degree. The same procedure is followed once he graduates with a BA or a BS and wishes to pursue a Masters degree, which is offered only at the Ramsey I unit, by the University of Houston-Clear Lake.

TDCJ does not itself offer college. It allows eleven two-year and three four-year universities and colleges to offer college courses, which are taught at twenty-five units. (See the Unit Profiles appendix to see which units offer college courses.) TDCJ provides the space for these classes. Since there are a limited number of inmates who can pay for and qualify for college, the curriculum is also limited. The esoteric electives offered on most campuses are not available in prison, but the basics assuredly are.

Most college courses are held in the WSD classrooms and are conducted during the evening hours. The instructors recognize the limitations that inmate/students face—no computers, very limited library resources, limited areas in which to study quietly—and thus don't require much of the outside reading and long, heavily researched papers that outside colleges do. This doesn't mean that the courses are cakewalks.

The many schools that offer two-year degrees and the three colleges that offer four-year degrees—Sam Houston State University, Tarleton State University, and the University of Houston-Clear Lake—pride themselves on their high standards. I have had many instructors tell me that in comparison with their free-world students, prison students are more attentive, more courteous, and make overall better grades. Of course, prison students don't have many of the distractions that free-world students have, but the degree requirements are the same, and the graduation ceremonies are full of proud students and their families.

TDCJ allows students to take correspondence courses, so long as the student complies with all mail regulations and the warden allows the course of instruction. Any inmate wanting to take correspondence courses should first contact the Continuing Education officer at his unit and acquaint himself with unit policy. However, any correspondence courses must be paid for by the student, and all arrangements, including registration, degree plans, etc., must be taken care of by the student or his family. The only thing TDCJ will do is provide a space for testing and a proctor to give the exams, usually the law library supervisor in the law library.

CHAPTER SEVENTEEN

discipline

One of the most famous judges in Texas history was Roy Bean, re-membered as the Law West of the Pecos as a result of the outrageous brand of justice he administered in Langtry, Texas. Judge Bean would ask miscreants how much money they had and then fine them exactly that much. He once ordered a hanged and buried criminal dug up and hanged again. Judge Bean would have fit in fine as a TDCJ disciplinary captain. The ultimate in frustration and helplessness felt by an inmate is when he goes before the Unit Disciplinary Committee and is steamrolled and flattened by the prison disciplinary machine.

The system seems simple, and maybe even just, to outsiders, if only because it mirrors the court system in the free-world. When inmates enter TDCJ, they are handed a book with the rules they must follow. If a guard believes an inmate has violated a rule, the guard writes a case—a ticket, if you will—that details the incident. The inmate is advised of the charges, and, depending on their seriousness, is appointed a substitute counsel, which is another guard, to aid in his defense. The inmate then appears before the Unit Disciplinary Committee, which is in reality a lone captain whose duties are to be the arm of justice on that unit. The inmate is allowed to present a defense, to call witnesses, and to appeal the findings. If found guilty, punishment is assessed from a range designed to fit the seriousness of the offense.

Seemingly simple, the system is so unfair and unjust that in my opinion, it defies belief. The major, and likely uncorrectable, flaw in it is the idea that in *all* situations the inmate is lying, the officer is not, and the inmate deserves whatever punishment he receives anyway. The punishment imposed can have long-lasting effects—on class, custody, parole eligibility, and on an inmate's release. I'm going to examine the disciplinary system by breaking it down—into the rules themselves, the guards' role, the Committee, and the inmates' role.

The Rules

The Texas Department of Corrections once had a rule called Disrespectful Attitude. It was left to the guards to determine which attitudes were sufficiently respectful or not. As you can imagine, any inmate who walked, talked, or even looked at a guard in a remotely challenging way was given a case. This rule was struck down by the courts in *Ruiz v. Estelle* as being too ambiguous, but its mere existence, and the guards' willingness to abuse it, exemplifies what is wrong about TDCJ rules.

To have moral force, a rule must serve a definite purpose. It must be clear. Those who break it must be punished in a like manner. If these conditions are not present, the rule and its enforcement are merely demonstration of power—do this or I will punish you because I can, and I will not punish another person because I don't want to. While many of the TDCJ rules are clear and purposeful, far too many are vague and contradictory, are meant to cover all possible situations, and are left to the officers' interpretations.

TDCJ rules are broken into four categories—Level I, Level II, Level III, and safety regulations. The categories are grouped by the severity of punishment that can be imposed. The system has a range of punishment at its disposal, which includes:

1. Loss of good time—this can result in a discharge date or parole eligibility being delayed for years. Some sentences demand that inmates serve a certain amount of their sentence before becoming eligible for parole. However, the majority doesn't—eligibil-

ity for parole and discharge is determined by a combination of flat time plus good time. Loss of good time pushes back both dates.

2. Reduction in good-time earning class—this has the same effect as above, in addition to requiring that satisfactory reviews precede any promotions to good-time earning class of the previous level. The lower class you are, the less good time you receive and the longer it takes to build eligibility for parole. Also, most educational and rehab programs require inmates to be in a certain class. A drop below that means that you will be dropped from educational classes and rehab programs, if enrolled, or not allowed to take any for at least a year from that date, and until you are again promoted.

3. Solitary—exactly what it says: a prescribed stay in solitary confinement, usually at least fifteen days.

4. Loss of recreation privileges—this means an inmate is not allowed to go to the gym, dayroom, law library, church, or attend any of the programmatic activities available. He must stay in his cell or cubicle unless at chow, or in the shower. This is usually assigned from fifteen to forty-five days, and it may be stacked up to ninety days.

5. Loss of commissary privileges—this means an inmate is not allowed to buy anything from the commissary for the amount of time this is assessed, usually fifteen to forty-five days.

6. Extra duty—inmates assessed extra duty must perform work in addition to their regularly assigned job. They are usually called out late in the evenings or at night and perform some sort of dirty, manual labor.

7. An accompanying, untallied punishment is a drop in custody level, which means that a minimum custody inmate drops to medium custody and a medium custody inmate drops to close custody. The lower in custody, the less privileges you have, and the more restricted environment you are in. In addition, officers are much more likely to write cases for trivial offenses in the lower custody classes, meaning it is much harder to get promoted back to minimum custody.

The case in classified as major if the punishment imposed is loss of good time, reduction in class, or solitary confinement. If charged with a Level I offense, there is no limit on the good time you can lose or the number of classes you can be dropped.

As you would expect, Level I offenses are fairly serious. They include escape, fighting with a weapon, assaulting an officer, rioting, inciting a riot, and any act the state defines as a felony. The purpose of Level I rules are clear—to maintain order. Level II and III offenses are less serious, and the punishment range is more restricted. Level II convictions may result in inmates losing no more than two years good time and a drop of no more than two levels in class. For Level III offenses an inmate can lose only one year of good time and be dropped only one class. However, the parole board will not consider an inmate for parole if he has been convicted of a major case within the last year, and *any* rules violation can be classified major. The reality is that any officer can always find an inmate in violation of something, because the Level II and III offenses are so broad that they can be interpreted in almost any way. Compounding this confusion, every unit has its own policy, set out by the warden, as to what is considered serious and to be strictly and what is trivial and thus to be ignored or tolerated.

For example, on the units with a concentration of younger inmates, fighting is expected, sometimes even encouraged by lower-ranking officers as a way of releasing tension. Inmates who fight will usually be ordered to shake hands and asked if the situation has been dealt with. They will only be given a case if they fight again, use a weapon, or fight in front of ranking officers. On other units it is expected that fights inevitably lead to retaliation and will escalate into stabbings or riots. Fighting on those units is not tolerated at all.

Another example—socks and t-shirts are sold in the commissary. The unit laundry does not wash personal items. It follows that inmates must be allowed to wash and dry those items somewhere. Since inmates do not have access to washers and dryers, they wash their clothes in the shower or in the cell. They then rig temporary lines in order to hang those items so they can dry. However, officers often write cases for inmates who hang clotheslines in their cells. The officers justify this by saying that the items used as clotheslines, usually shoelaces, were bought or issued for tying one's shoes, and are being used for an unauthorized purpose, hanging clothes. Officers will write a case for Unauthorized Use, confiscate the clotheslines, and sometimes the drying clothes. This is petty, of course, but it is also common on the newer units. The fact that using shoelaces to dry clothes does not threaten security is of no relevance.

One more example—access to the craft shop is highly prized and tightly restricted on most units. However, TDCJ allows "in-cell piddling" for minor crafts, usually art, whereby inmates can make cards or portraits and sell them to each other. On many units, this is not only allowed, it is encouraged, because staff would rather have inmates busy drawing and not fighting. It also allows inmates the opportunity to make a little money and not have to scrounge and steal in order to have a few luxuries.

But many units do not allow in-cell piddling whatsoever, and any inmate having a felt pen, a red or green ink pen (not sold in the commissary), or any type of cardboard for making cards will be given a major case for possession of contraband. What is more infuriating is that an inmate may be transferred from a unit where piddling is allowed to a unit where it is not. If he doesn't know this—and it is never posted or part of the orientation process—once an officer finds the art equipment in the inmate's possession, no amount of argument will prevent him from receiving a case, possible major, for simply acting in a fashion that was perfectly legal, even encouraged, just a few miles down the road.

Not only are unit interpretations of rules contradictory, the rules themselves are. Inmates are ordered to keep their cells and living areas clean and can in fact be given cases for failure to do so. However, many units do not issue any type of cleanser or soap. So, if an inmate has bleach or cleanser in his possession, even for the benign purpose of cleaning his cell or washing his clothes —what else can you do with the stuff?—he must have stolen them and will be given a case for either Stealing State Property or Possession of Contraband, or maybe both. If an inmate has a rag, it is assumed he has ripped it from a sheet or shirt, and he is then given a case for Destruction of State Property. He is expected to clean his cell with the towel he is issued to dry himself with after he washes his face—his cell towel so becomes his broom, mop, and rag.

There are two rules that were created to take the place of the late Disrespectful Attitude. One is Creating Unnecessary Noise, which is whatever an officer says it is, at any level, including a whisper and in one case I personally know of, a burp during count. The other is Failure to complete a Reasonable Amount of Work. Reasonable is left to the officer to define, and if he says it is reasonable and you don't do it, you've got a case. Of course, since "reasonable" has no measurable quality, and we all have different capabilities, what one can do as reasonable is unreasonable for another. But that argument carries no weight with a TDCJ disciplinary captain. Since every officer is allowed to define what is reasonable to him, there is no set rule, no way to comply, and you are always guilty.

Officers

Let's examine the officers' role in this. Officers are human. Prison dehumanizes all who come into it, and officers are no exception. Some are lenient and easygoing. They retain their sanity by treating prison as a game. They speak of doing their eight hours and going home. Some guards are distant and by the book. They treat inmates as non-feeling objects to be managed without emotion. Many of the lower ranking officers—the sergeants and lieutenants—adopt this attitude. A few officers are brutal and cruel. They lie every bit as much as inmates do, and they gravitated to their jobs for the power it affords them.

This last group of guards—as most seasoned correctional professionals will readily admit—is the cause of most of the frustration, animosity, and inmate-on-guard violence in prison. These guards are usually young, insecure, and afraid. After all, they are in a violent environment, where intimidation is the norm. To retain control, these guards believe they must dominate the inmates. Since they cannot do this physically—convicts outnumber them and are men who have demonstrated a willingness to brutalize others—the guards use what they have been given: their pencils. These guards look for small infractions. When an inmate protests over the petty nature of a case, the guards will upgrade what was a minor rule infraction into a major confrontation. And in any major confrontation, the officer, backed by the power of the state and an approving public, will always win and thus validate his power.

Let me make this clear. Officers are always right. *Always.* An officer can do what he wishes to an inmate, and regardless of the inmate witnesses, of the inmate's possible clean disciplinary record and reputation as a quiet, responsible, rules-abiding convict and of the officer's possible reputation as a lying bully; the officer's version of the event will be the *official* version of the event. Maybe everyone involved knew the inmate was right—and perhaps, off the record, they *told* the inmate he was right—but he will receive a case and be punished. TDCJ guards have killed inmates, and it was only through free-world intervention that those officers were punished, because within the system an inmate's word carries no weight whatsoever.

I'll give two examples. There are rules against sexual misconduct. While any sexual activity in Texas prisons is illegal, this rule is enforced only (other than in clear homosexual conduct) by female officers or staff members who charge inmates with exposure meant to "gain sexual gratification," as the rulebook quaintly puts it. There are undoubtedly many convicts who do this; in fact, there is an entire convict subculture, comprised of what are called "gunslingers," who tell each other which female guard will not write a case on a convict who exposes himself to her and masturbates while she is in the vicinity. These men do, indeed, gain sexual gratification from exposure.

However, any convict who is accused of this will automatically be found guilty, and there are some female guards who take advantage of this and retaliate against inmates who have angered them in some fashion. If an inmate argues with a female guard one day in the hall, she may go back to the picket, say he exposed himself to her while she was counting, and he will lose class, good time, be dropped a custody level and have to explain to the parole board why he is now a sexual offender.

Another example. One of the Level I offenses is Assault on an Officer, which also carries a free-world penalty, if convicted, of at least a twenty-five-year sentence. By TDCJ's calculations, in 1997 there were 1,442 inmate assaults on guards. As there were only 1,499 inmate-on-inmate assaults during the same period, this means inmates assaulted guards with the same frequency they did each other. This is ridiculous. Many of these "assaults" were just that. But many were also the result of 1) inmates spitting on or toward guards, 2) inmates bumping into guards, and 3) inmates who assumed threatening postures against guards. By this I mean that if I argue with a guard and wave my arms, he and two other guards will tackle me, then charge me with Assault on an Officer to justify their use of force.

The bad guards lie, the indifferent ones wink, and the good ones—whom are undoubtedly in the majority—will turn away, compelled by the same code that allows police officers to cover up for each others' transgressions. I once had a supervisor, a good, caring, Christian man, tell me that he would always side with the officer in a dispute with an inmate. This was on a unit where three guards had just been indicted for manslaughter after lying for months about an inmate's death. That same officer told me the unit warden had decreed that if a guard initiated a case against an inmate, the case would *always* be graded major and the inmate *always* found guilty. This lieutenant was telling me that no due process whatsoever existed on that unit; that the officers had a green light to give any case they wanted; that the Unit Disciplinary Committee was a total farce; that it had been for years; and that regardless, he would still side with any officer over any inmate.

The Committee

Any time a guard thinks an inmate has broken a rule, he is advised to seek informal resolution if applicable. If not, he is supposed to ask the inmate for his ID card, advise him that he is writing a case, write a report, and submit it to his supervisor, who will then investigate the incident and decide if it should be submitted for review.

If it is graded minor, a lieutenant will hold an informal hearing and punish the inmate with some sort of restriction and perhaps a few hours of extra duty. If the case is graded major, it will be given to a substitute counsel, who is merely a guard who has opted out of the general population and been trained in the disciplinary procedures. (I do not mean legal training. I have never met a substitute counsel who knew more than the bare rudiments about the law, not even the relevant cases that have established due process rights of prisoners. The substitute counsels are still under the direct supervision of the building major—who usually grades the cases—and are subject to his and the warden's orders and discipline.)

The counsel will then interview the inmate, take his statement, contact any witnesses, and be in the courtroom with the inmate and the captain who will conduct the hearing itself. The hearing is recorded, or at least the parts the captain wants are recorded. (I have been in hearings where the tape recorder—ordered by the federal courts to preserve the hearing for appeal—was turned off by a captain so he could curse and threaten off the record.) There is a formula to the hearings, which most captains will follow. They will ask the inmate to give a statement and to submit what documents he has prepared. Although an inmate has the right to confront the accusing officer, this rarely happens, the captain satisfying himself with a statement. Sometimes, the captain will call the officer on the telephone, say the inmate has alleged this or that, ask the officer what he has to say, and enter into the record the officer's statement.

After taking into account the officer's statement, whatever evidence both sides offered and other relevant factors—the inmate's disciplinary record, the severity of the offense—the captain will pronounce judgment. I should say, rather, the captain will announce punishment, because rarely, if ever, will the inmate be found innocent. He must overwhelmingly prove total incompetence on the part of the charging officer to stand any chance, and then the case will be dropped to minor. The sad truth is that once an inmate has been charged with an offense in a Texas prison, the only question left to address is the severity of punishment.

This may sound like an exaggeration. But I've known inmates not get cases for eight, nine, or ten years, work in responsible jobs and have outstanding reputations, yet when they are accused of something and go to court, regardless of their defense, they are found guilty, lose good time, and class—all because one officer didn't like their attitude.

The only way to win is to not let the case get to the hearing stage. An inmate who has been around a long time is usually friendly with at least some ranking officers, with someone who will try to have the case pulled before it goes to the major for grading. Officers know this, so they'll sometimes hold the paperwork back on a particular inmate they want to bust, then give the case to a ranking officer who does not get along with the officer friendly with the inmate. It's political, as it is in the free-world, except that the consequences for the inmate can mean more years in prison.

I once went to breakfast, was given a tablespoon of peanut butter and tried to take it to my cell to eat with crackers. A guard stopped me on the way to the block, searched me, found the peanut butter and threw it in the trash. I accused him of being petty. He wrote me up for Stealing State Property. I lost six months good time, was dropped in class, and received a year set-off by the parole board, which means the incident cost me a year in prison. A photo of the peanut butter was taken as evidence, which the warden later showed my wife as proof of my bad character.

There may be in TDCJ a warden who wants a disciplinary captain to conduct fair hearings. There may be a disciplinary captain fair enough to question an officer's version of an event and to believe an inmate's version. There may be a substitute counsel who will do other than advise an inmate to plead guilty and avoid harsher punishment. But I haven't met any, nor have I heard of any.

The Inmates' Role

Now, for the bitter truth. In my opinion many disciplinary cases arise from situations where an officer harasses an inmate and the inmate refuses to give in, out or pride, or anger, or peer pressure, or sometimes just stupidity. Inmates know that some officers will take any opportunity to exercise their authority. They believe the substitute counsels are a joke. They know the disciplinary captains and the wardens are more concerned with security than fairness, are not concerned if an inmate loses years of good time over an officer's possible lie, and in fact would prefer that to happen than take the inmate's word over an officer's and risk alienating the officers, especially when confronted with staff shortages.

Inmates know the disciplinary system is a farce and corrupt and that it exists in Texas only because Judge William Wayne Justice ordered the state to provide a semblance of due process. Yet, in our anger and unwillingness to just shut up, we give the system a chance to practice its evil on us.

The fact is, I didn't have to take that peanut butter to my cell. Once I was caught, I didn't have to complain—I knew the officer was trying to build a reputation as a hardass. I placed myself in front of the steam-roller with my actions, as do most of us. We can decide to do our time quietly, studying and working, and not hang pictures in our cells. We can avoid the guards, and say, "Yes, Sir" and "No, Sir," and simply let those guards believe they are as bad as they want us to believe. None of this wounds us or makes us bleed, or does anything other than hurt our prison pride, or our false dignity, something we need to discard and replace with a sense of responsibility for our actions. In short, we cannot control the guards and we cannot change the system, not through anger. We can fight, within the system, within the law, quietly and with reason. But we must accept that we are here, the great majority of us, because of our own actions. We must not allow the disciplinary system the satisfaction of breaking us and our hopes.

CHAPTER EIGHTEEN

lockdowns

*R*arely does TDCJ label anything so accurately. A lockdown is just that—every inmate in the locked-down wing, block, dorm, or unit is confined to his cell or cubicle, with no movement, no work, no recreation, no school, no visit, and with sometimes only cold sack lunches to eat for weeks on end. Lockdowns may last from hours to months and are imposed by wardens for different reasons. Although the ranking officer on duty has the authority to order a lockdown, anything lasting more than a few hours and affecting more than a few inmates will be ordered by a warden, and it must be justified to the regional and system directors.

Some wardens order lockdowns every six months or so to search the unit for tobacco, drugs, or weapons. These lockdowns are usually in the middle of the week, last only twenty-four to seventy-two hours, and do not disrupt visiting schedules. Many inmates welcome these lockdowns, as they offer three-day vacations from work. However, if a unit is plagued by continual violence, or if a riot is believed imminent, officials will order a lockdown that may last from a seventy-two-hour cooling off period to months. These longer lockdowns usually are on close-custody wings, where more violent inmates are concentrated.

For whatever reason a lockdown is ordered, it begins with all inmates ordered to their cells or cubicles. If it is a unit-wide lockdown, staff will make sack lunches, or "Johnnies," for the inmates' meals. (A Johnny consists of two sandwiches—a peanut butter and jelly sandwich and a bologna sandwich—and a piece of cake or pack of raisins. Inmates on extended lockdowns lose quite a bit of weight.) Everything is suspended—no showering, no change of clothes, no leaving your cell until a decision is made to lift the lockdown or formally extend it. After a few days of investigating the disturbance that initiated the lockdown, and after a shakedown to reaffirm the guards' authority, the areas not involved in the disturbance are allowed to resume normal activities. If necessary, inmates will be moved from block to block in order to isolate those deemed likely to continue the behavior that initiated the lockdown. The others, usually minimum or medium custody inmates, are allowed to resume their duties, without which the unit cannot function for long.

If a decision is made to maintain a lockdown, the inmates involved are placed on a four-week schedule, with privileges gradually returned. Initially, inmates will be allowed showers three times a week, be given clean clothes only then, and will eat only Johnnies. All regular activities cease. All privileges are suspended. Visits are not allowed until the third week. Commissary privileges are totally suspended for the first two weeks, and resume with a ten dollar hygiene spend on the third week. Hot meals, once a day, are not resumed until the third week. Depending on the warden's review, full privileges and rights will be restored when he believes they are warranted by the inmates' behavior. I have been on lockdowns where week one was repeated for a month when an inmate cursed an officer or yelled out of a window. Some wardens use lockdowns as a way of starving rebellious inmates into obeying.

An integral part of a lockdown is a shakedown, which is a concentrated search for contraband. While that is a justifiable concern in prison, rarely does a shakedown find weapons or drugs in an inmate's property. Once the doors are locked, and it is apparent that a shakedown is imminent, contraband is discarded.

Shakedowns are exercises in control. Take all you own and toss it on a sheet. (Imagine being able to toss all your worldly possessions onto a sheet!) Drag it a quarter-mile to the shakedown area. Strip and let a guard look into your mouth, between your toes, and into all your body cavities. Stand there naked while officers with life and death power over you toss your belongings back onto the sheet—talcum powder drifting over your college paperwork, sodas leaking onto your photographs—and the guards taking what they wish, advising you to write a grievance if you don't like their treatment.

The charged atmosphere of shakedowns often results in violence, but shakedowns, and lockdowns, allow prisons to reassert control by demonstrating exactly who is in charge.

The sudden nature of lockdowns should reinforce something I suggested in the chapter on visits: *call* a few days before visiting, especially if you are driving hundreds of miles. If the unit was locked down on Thursday, and if the lockdown continues throughout the weekend, you will not be allowed to have a visit with anyone, even if they have not personally broken any rules, until the lockdown is lifted. I repeat, *call* before visiting.

CHAPTER NINETEEN

drugs

*I*n March of 1995, TDCJ outlawed the use of tobacco products on all of its units, by both guards and inmates. Trumpeted as a cost-saving measure, the move probably did save the system millions of dollars. Building interiors no longer needed the constant repainting due to layers of smoke scum. The damage done by incidental, and sometimes intentional, fires was eliminated. Convicts suffering from asthma, emphysema, and other lung ailments could literally breathe easier, and convicts' health improved overall, dropping the system's medical cost.

One totally unintended consequence of the new tobacco policy was a sharp decline in drug trafficking, as the convicts who sold drugs—and the guards who smuggled them—realized the enormous profits and relatively low risks of now trafficking tobacco. While drugs are still available—especially on the units where older convicts retain their lifelong addiction to heroin—the businessmen who maintained the large operations now deal tobacco, not cocaine or marijuana.

The truth in this is borne out by a recent study that said that random drug analyses of convicts in all fifty states showed that Texas led the nation in drug-free tests, with ninety-eight percent of those tested coming up clean. TDCJ officials attributed this to the fact that TDCJ no longer has inmates going on furloughs and thus inmates can no longer bring in drugs, and that is undoubtedly part of the reason Texas convicts are so clean. But the other is the fact the tobacco black market is so lucrative that it makes drug smuggling incredibly stupid.

For years, drugs in prison were dealt by two groups: the addicted and the connected. Sometimes, these were the same, as addicts coming into the system kept their free-world connections and established pipelines for the flow of heroin, cocaine, and marijuana. But no one deals in prison without gang sponsorship, or at least approval. Stronger on some units but present on all, the gangs take a piece of each delivery and eventually take control of the mules—the inmate trusties and the guards.

But drug dealing is essentially about money. The addict who deals eventually cannot maintain his business, as he uses up his profits or allows his need to push him into bad decisions. The dealer who doesn't use his product deals strictly for profit. While drug dealing is a profitable business, the risks are huge, especially in prison, where there are few diversions and nowhere to run. Not only are prison officials out to bust you, so are local, state, and federal law enforcement agencies. One sale to an informant can result in a lengthy sentence stacked on the one now being done. For the guards, arrest for smuggling will result in their being placed among a group of men who abhor all law enforcement personnel and are ready to prove it.

But so long as there was money to be made and no black market alternative, drugs were readily available, because the gangs had members ready to be plugged into the slots of those getting arrested.

At one time, inhalants were a big business. When the guards were more scarce and rarely ventured onto the runs, glue and thinner were big sellers. But the increase of officers and their correspondingly greater presence in inmate living quarters has put a damper on inhalant abuse. You'll still see pockets of thinner sniffers, usually on the yard at night, telltale by the rags or empty Coke cans held to their noses. These cheap-thrill addicts buy thinner from maintenance workers or craft shop members, gas from transportation workers, and correction fluid from clerks.

Now the money is in tobacco, which is just as profitable with much less risk. One cigarette sells for up to two dollars, depending on the unit and the type of money—"good money" being food or coffee, "junk money" being anything else. One pack of tobacco yields forty to sixty cigarettes. That pack will cost a dealer ten dollars in cash, usually smuggled in during a visit and then given to a guard. In turn, the guard will take that ten dollars, buy six or eight packs of tobacco, and sell each pack for ten dollars to his prison dealer. So, the dealer turned ten dollars into seventy or so dollars worth of prison goods, while the guard turned the ten into seventy dollars worth of tobacco. And lest you think it's totally penny ante, I will assure you that there are plenty of convicts who smoke all week on credit, then go to the store, spend seventy-five dollars on food and hand every bit of it to their cigarette connection. It's a nice market, and the local district attorney, sheriff, and Drug Enforcement Agency agents couldn't care less.

Smoking is done furtively. Inmates smoke in their cells, one watching for guards while the other puffs away, exhaling into the toilet, flushing, and hoping most of the smoke is carried into the pipes. In dorms, an inmate may take a cigarette into the shower, smoking until it gets wet and falls apart. Many inmates smoke at work, especially in industrial shops where many supervisors are themselves smokers and turn a blind eye. As long as the smoking is not too overt, many supervisors ignore it. A few security officers will also ignore the smoker, but most will not, and a few will write disciplinary cases on any nearby inmates if the officer even smells smoke.

Since both matches and lighters are contraband, ingenious methods are used to light cigarettes. Usually, two pieces of pencil lead are placed into an electrical outlet, one in each socket. Another piece of lead is touched to the two, and the resulting spark is enough to ignite a slip of toilet paper. This burning paper will be used to light a few cigarettes. Often, doing this will overload the electrical circuits, causing fans, televisions, and radios to shut down. Non-smokers are often angry at the nuisances caused by the smoking inmates.

A convict who gets caught with a cigarette—or with ten packs—will get a major case and lose class, status, and good time, but doesn't face any free-world penalty. Neither does the guard. After all, tobacco is still legal. The guard will most likely be fired, but faces no legal consequences. Not all tobacco is smuggled in by guards, of course, just as not all drugs are. Ingenious convicts will have tobacco sent in via any well-known courier, in boxes meant for industry warehouses and then intercepted by convict shipping clerks. Or they'll have it sent in with the bread trucks, driven through the back gate, and unloaded on the kitchen docks. Or they'll have it dropped in packets on some lonely back road, to be picked up by outside trusties, out at 4 A.M. to round up cattle. But by far the most is brought in by guards. The money is too good; the smuggling is too easy; and the risks are too small. There is a movement to try to have the Legislature make a felony of this, or at least a heavy misdemeanor, but it remains to be seen if it can get pushed through.

This has left drug smuggling to the hardcore addicts, who deal enough to support their habits and nothing more. The average convict can, by persistent questioning and enough money, find a shot of heroin or a match-box of marijuana. But it's an extremely hard buy. The dealers aren't actively looking for customers, who represent merely another possibility of arrest. The drugs that come in now are usually already bought and paid for, reserved for long-time customers—the addicted, close-mouthed convicts with money and reputations for never divulging their sources.

CHAPTER TWENTY

racism, riots, and gangs

A *Time* cover story in the early 1980's declared the East Texas prison unit of Eastham "America's Toughest Prison," a distinction hotly disputed by other Texas prison units. The entire then-Texas Department of Corrections rocked after Judge William Wayne Justice ordered the building tender system dismantled as a result of *Ruiz v. Estelle*. Without its inmate goons to keep order, TDC was exposed as almost criminally understaffed.

Coupled with the mass resignings and reassignments of many old-time guards and wardens—who had flourished under Director W.J. Estelle's term—the lack of supervision left a power vacuum that was soon exploited by burgeoning prison gangs. Flexing their muscles, the various gangs waged war for the right to control the prison drug trade and jumped at the opportunity to settle old scores. The murder rates rocketed as the media fueled the killing frenzy by publicly lamenting the records for violent deaths that TDCJ convicts were daily rewriting. Clemens, Ellis, I, Coffield, Ramsey I, Darrington—where a 1984 triple murder in a sunlit dayroom prompted TDC's first system-wide lockdown as officials frantically tried to isolate gang members—all laid valid claims to the dubious title of America's deadliest joint.

As prison officials gradually identified gang leaders, isolated them in administrative segregation, and took back the cellblocks, the death rates dropped. The violence didn't and unfortunately never will. The Texas prison system is now more violent, more racist, and more brutal than it ever was. An influx of young convicts with unimaginably long sentences has created an atmosphere where respect and reputation rarely come into play, and the resulting brutality is more pervasive than ever and contributes to an environment that stifles hope and positive growth of any kind. While it is not as deadly in TDCJ as it once was, it is not because convicts aren't assaulting one another. There are a few reasons for the drop in deaths.

First, weapons aren't nearly as available. Through the mid-1980s, material for homemade knives was everywhere. The chow halls offered metal spoons. The commissary sold metal fans, and an enterprising convict could fashion dozens of shanks (makeshift knives) from the blade and grill of one fan. Inmates were constantly armed with foot-long, razor-sharp weapons. Now, even officers eat with plastic cutlery, and the few pieces of scrap iron in prison kitchens and laundries are tagged and disposed of—at least on the more violence-plagued units. While a determined inmate can still get his hands on a good weapon—a screwdriver or a honed piece of angle iron from the Maintenance Department—most shanks are short, light, and incapable of killing, unless one hits an eye or throat.

Second, the enormous increase of guards means that TDCJ has the manpower to search convicts in a way not possible before. In 1980, two officers controlled a wing of four blocks, overseeing from 750-800 inmates, albeit with a number of building tenders. Now, five to six guards run a wing—one or two on each block, two in the pickets and two turning keys. There are guards on each gate, utility officers roaming hallways or gathered around phones and desks. On units with a preponderance of young inmates, where violence is common, there are enough guards to stripsearch inmates every time they enter the blocks or the recreation areas, especially on medium and close custody areas.

Third, the penalties for assault and murder are much higher. Inmates used to kill each other and receive five and ten-year sentences, if they were prosecuted at all. The attitude used to be, "Let them kill one another." While that attitude may still be paramount, there also exists a separate district attorney who does nothing but prosecute inmate offenders. It is a capital offense for an inmate to kill another as part of a gang-related hit. Also, all sentences assessed a convict for felonies committed while in prison are stacked on the one he is serving, essentially meaning he must be granted parole on the first, or accumulate enough time to discharge it, before he even begins to amass credit on the second sentence.

Accordingly, while the prison population skyrocketed from 39,000 in 1988 to 64,000 in 1993 to a mind-boggling 139,000 in 1997, the homicide rate has not kept pace—from a low of three in 1988 to nine in 1987. The numbers are nowhere near the fifty to sixty yearly murders committed in TDC from 1983 to 1986.

I want to comment on the statistics I'll use in this chapter. They were obtained—except for the 1983-1986 homicides—from the TDCJ public information office. However, every statistic can be skewed by over and under-reporting. The Texas prison system is infamous for telling you what it wants you to know and not telling you what it doesn't want you to know. For instance, TDCJ claims there were 1,449 offender assaults in 1997, roughly three per day. Think about this. Almost 140,000 of the roughest, meanest men in Texas, not having to worry about being shot in retaliation, had less assaults than a Texas city of comparable size. This is absurd. What it reflects is the way assaults are defined by TDCJ.

If five convicts take turns beating another almost to death, for money or gang purposes or mere sport, and use only their hands and fists, TDCJ will call it a simple fight, deal with it administratively and not enter it into its assault statistics. However, TDCJ also claims that during the same period there were 1,442 inmate-on-staff assaults. Understand this: if an inmate spits toward a guard, it is defined as assault, and free-world charges can and likely will be assessed the inmate. Therefore, the level of violence necessary for the two assault charges is extremely different. Thus are the inmate-on-inmate assaults kept low and the inmate-on-staff assaults artificially high.

Also, the number of suicides—TDCJ admits to seventeen in 1997—undoubtedly hides a number of homicides, and is also kept low through the existence of a strange statistical category: Self Mutilation. TDCJ counted 682 accounts of Self Mutilation in 1997. What differentiates those from the Attempted Suicides, of which there were 628 in 1997? The level of blood spilled? The severity of the cut? Perhaps just a desire to not admit how many desperate men—at least 1,310 in 1997— were willing to cut themselves and die rather than to live behind these walls? I will give you a reason why—TDCJ does not admit to *any* sexual assaults within its walls. *None.*

Free-world journalists have asked and been told the numbers are not "readily available." Yet each TDCJ unit has, in its infirmary, rape kits to allow doctors to collect evidence of sexual assaults. And, to quote from *Ruiz v. Johnson,* 37 F. Supp. 2d 855, page 917.

> "No attempt is made to monitor the total number of reported sexual assaults in TDCJ, and the result is that differing accounts are extant concerning the total number of sexual assaults. In 1997 there were eighty-seven reported sexual assaults. However, in a letter written by TDCJ Executive Services, the number is 'approximately 123' for the year of 1997. According to the first document, in 1998 there were eighty-one reported sexual assaults. Yet another number reveals that in 1998, there were 107 reported sexual assaults that were examined by the internal Affairs Division. . . . There are a number of plausible reasons why the number of reported sexual assaults are so low in a prison system that has a population of 140,000. For example, according to Deputy Director of Security Janie Cockrell, [now Institutional Division Director] male inmates have difficulty reporting sexual assaults. An additional, perhaps alternative, explanation for the low reporting of sexual assaults lies in the fact that the system does not encourage victims to come forward and complain about the sexual crimes perpetrated against them. First, there appears to be a strong presumption on the part of prison officials that, in the absence of outward physical harm to assaulted inmates such as cuts, abrasions, and bruises, no sexual assault has occurred. Second, according to the testimony of inmates, those who report that they have been raped are subjected to disdain by officers. Third, with only six disciplinary actions

for sexual abuse in 1998 for the entire prison population, there
appear to have been no serious ramifications for those inmates
committing sexual assault against other inmates. Indeed, there
is apparently little concern that six confirmed sexual assaults
for 1998 might not accurately reflect what is actually occurring
in Texas prisons."

So, while TDCJ would say to a journalist that statistics concerning
sexual assault were not "readily available," it would say something entirely different to the courts. Take the statistics as you wish. I give them
to you as they were presented to me, yet from experience I believe inmate-on-inmate violence is vastly underreported, as are sexual assaults
and attempted suicides. While violent death in TDCJ has abated, violence has not. The two main causes are what you'd expect—racism and
intergang warfare.

Violence has always been a part of prison. At one time, however, it
was fairly predictable. Every man was tested when he first came to the
joint. Either his homeboys called him out and took him on, one by one,
until it was decided he had "heart," or he was attacked by a group and
judged on how violently he fought back against overwhelming odds. There
was always a certain percentage of men who would not fight, or were
paralyzed by fear, and those men were "turned out," or raped and sold
back and forth, with most of the trade being controlled by building tenders, now by gangs.

In any event, after the initial burst of bloody violence, if a convict
responded with courage, he was usually left alone and had to almost ask
for trouble. It came unbidden to the usual suspects—those who drank,
did drugs, gambled, dallied in homosexual affairs, traded on the black
market, or otherwise danced on the line between what was *my* business
or *your* business."Business" is a sacred yet hard-to-define aspect of prison.
Convicts have so little to call their own, and so little privacy, that they
fiercely retaliate against infringements on personal space and activities.
A man who walks by a cell and looks into it with more than a quick
glance is quickly challenged with "You got any business in here?" A
man who comments, unasked, on a conversation between two others is
considered to be meddling, accused of "burglarizing another's conver-

sation," and can expect to be challenged. *My* business is anything I own, anything I do, anything I plan, and I have the right to own it, sell it, destroy it, to plan, converse, connive, and conspire, without having another inmate comment or intrude on my activities.

Once a man proved himself and showed he was respectful of another's business, he was left alone, unless he somehow ran afoul of the guards. Acquiring a reputation as a writ writer, who agitated for prisoners' civil rights, was sure to land a convict on the guards' hit list. Falling out of official favor meant incurring the wrath of the building tenders. That group's brutality was the birthing agent of more than one gang, formed as a way to combat the man's feared flunkies. At least one prison gang promised the building tenders that if you kill one of us, two of you die.

The practice of using building tenders accomplished a few things, but foremost it allowed the system to save money, as they performed exactly the same duties that guards would—along with their janitorial duties, they counted, they turned keys, they participated in the assignment of cells, they passed out mail and medicine, and they stitched up wounds. In exchange for these duties, they were allowed almost limited freedom within the walls. Their cells were left open. They were allowed weapons—knives, clubs, chains, saps. They were shock troops, and in exchange for the privileges granted them they had to keep the other inmates in line and provide information on their activities. They were detested and feared, and TDCJ's upper management's adamant refusal to admit they had the power they did ultimately turned the tide in *Ruiz v. Estelle.*

By 1973, the legislature had expressly outlawed the use of prisoners to discipline others, yet Director W. J. Estelle refused to admit that the building tenders were other than janitors. However, a group of federal monitors appointed by Judge Justice to investigate the situation began preparing evidence that Estelle and his subordinates were lying to the court and to higher state officials. On March 15, 1982, two years after Justice had ruled in favor of the inmates in *Ruiz* and saw one order after another defied by Estelle and TDC, witnesses began to give testimony. The Board of Corrections finally agreed to do away with the building tenders. The loss of credibility that Estelle suffered doomed him and his regime, and from then on, Justice had his way with the Texas prison system and state officials.

Such was prison violence through the mid 1970s, when the state slowly began to integrate its units. Until that time, certain units were reserved for certain races. In the 1970s, Texas began to integrate its units while leaving living areas segregated. Even that fell by the wayside in the late 1970s, and the mixing of men who had never been together in groups resulted in riots throughout the system. One famous riot is referred to in *Ruiz v. Estelle,* a June 1978 riot on Ferguson, the day after the blocks where the field force lived were integrated. So uncommon and unprecedented was the commotion and craziness that Director Estelle himself showed up, ordered the inmates to desist, and when they refused, stood by as unit officials ordered such a barrage of gas and retaliatory brutality by guards and building tenders that the entire incident is wonderingly footnoted by Judge Justice as proof of prison officials' reliance on unnecessary use of force. (503 Fed. Supp. 1265, U.S. District Court, southern Division, TX, 1980, page 1301.)

But the racial violence always took a back seat to the savagery inflicted by gang members on their enemies, usually of the same race, and overwhelmingly Hispanic. Two rival Chicano gangs—the Mexican Mafia and the Texas Syndicate—warred throughout the 1980s and accounted for the majority of the homicides and blood spilled between gangs. Whatever they were fighting for is lost in the haze of recrimination and revenge, and TDCJ filled ad/seg with Hispanic warriors, identifying gang members by whichever method it found expedient.

By TDCJ's own figures, Hispanics constitute one-fourth of the overall population, yet Hispanic gang members make up almost three-fourths of all gang members locked up in ad/seg. This is testament to the blind ferocity displayed by the Hispanic gang members, and to the willingness of TDCJ officials to use any tattoo with Chicano/Aztec/cholo symbolism or incidental contact between suspected gang members as enough evidence to lock away Hispanics, something not done to Anglo or Black convicts. This is a sore point with many Hispanics, but perversely also a point of pride. Members of the Bloods and Crips, which are almost without exception Black, are not automatically assigned to ad/seg, the official reason being that they do not have written constitutions governing their activities. Neither, until very recently, were many members of the Anglo groups put into ad/seg, except for the Aryan Brotherhood, as the

Aryan Circle and White Knights attempt to portray themselves as quasi-religious organizations. While lamenting the official attitude that their gangs represent organized criminal organizations with free-world tentacles, which results in their being locked away, Hispanics prefer to believe it is because they are much more violent and dangerous than the other gangs.

There are at least eleven full-fledged gangs in Texas prisons and thousands of members and hangers-on roam the halls of the units. However, except for sporadic skirmishes between members of like-race gangs—and TDCJ officials will hotly dispute me on this—gangs are *not* the focal point of TDCJ violence. The gangs have adopted a wary peace. If a member of one group falls out with a member of another, one of two things will likely take place. Either the two inmates will be allowed to fight, with members of both groups watching to make sure no one interferes, or the offending members of each gang will be beaten by their own brothers. The gangs understand that they are watched closely, and if a member antagonizes another group and in the process brings heat on the whole structure, he will be "checked," or beaten, by his fellow gang members.

TDCJ officials will vehemently say that I am wrong, that the gangs are the root of almost all violence in Texas prisons. This is because such an analysis leads to a simple solution—build more super-security prisons for the gang members. I am convinced, however, after twenty-one years in prison and with an intimate understanding of the racial undercurrents here, that the gangs are not the main cause of Texas prison violence. That blame lies in the insidious racism that permeates prison and with the failure of the system to deal with it in any fashion but through forced integration.

The population of TDCJ has changed. It has become younger, and the new laws mandating that convicts serve a much longer percentage of their sentences before arriving at parole eligibility has created a sense of hopelessness among those younger convicts. They band together in groups based on geographic or racial similarities, and their allegiance is to each other. While they are usually not identified as gangs because they have neither written constitutions nor self-applied sobriquets, these groups are the focal point of much of the mindless brutality that exists in TDCJ, and most of it is directed against Anglos.

In almost every Texas prison, Latinos and Blacks group together in "tangos," or home-boy cliques, with an elected speaker. An affront to the dignity of their origin—be it a city, a country, or a vague aggregate of small towns, will result in group retaliation. (El West, for instance, is the stretch west of Dallas, including the Panhandle down to El Paso.) The group members will look out for each other, providing commissary essentials and backup in case one gets in trouble with other convicts.

These groups may war with each other, but one crucial difference between them and gangs is that a member can at any time go "solo" if he decides his group is led by ineffective leadership or if he just doesn't agree with the clique concept. Contrast this with the "blood in, blood out" mindset of the gangs, which demands a set length of time as a prospect, followed by violent proof of desire to join—a beating of an enemy, a stabbing or a death. Homeboys belonging to "tangos" are readily embraced, often merely on the word of a free-world friend. Some groups of individual units may demand an initiation, but it is not as formal or violent as gang initiation.

This sense of solidarity protects Latinos and Blacks from being preyed upon. For example—if a Latino is celled with a Black, and the Black is huge and consistently beats the Latino, as long as the Latino fights back, doesn't ask for help and is not being sexually assaulted, the situation will not escalate or change until 1) the Black gains respect for the Latino's heart and desists, 2) the Latino dies, or 3) the Latino attacks his tormentor with a weapon. If the Latino is broken, however, and the Black in any way says he is sexually assaulting him or taking his property, the Latino's homeboys will intervene.

The Latino prison code will not allow another Latino to "ride" with a Black, barring extraordinary circumstances, usually involving the Latino denying any desire to associate with Latinos at all. So, if pressed, whatever "tango" the Latino is from will rise up, confront the Black, tell him that while he may have broken the Latino he cannot have him, and that war awaits if he insists on keeping him. This proprietary interest is acknowledged by both groups and prevents many weaker inmates from being broken by members of other races.

However, Anglos don't usually ascribe to this code. White inmates don't group together by homeboys but by the heart that is displayed by each when he is challenged. And they will be challenged. Go on any unit in the system. Walk into any medium or close-custody block and, if you are white, you will be immediately called to defend yourself, over and over again, and sometimes even that will not be enough. On many units, the Blacks and Latino vow that "all white boys will ride," so an Anglo who fights back will face regular beatings by increasing numbers, until he is broken, moved, stabs someone and is put in ad/seg, or somehow convinces the other inmates to leave him alone.

So, the Anglos who have been in those situations—who have faced up to the beatings and refused to pay money or provide sex, have perhaps done time in ad/seg and worked their way into the general population, and maybe have shadowy affiliations with the white supremacist groups, or just stand alone—those Anglos take pride in calling themselves "peckerwoods" or "staydown woods" and have nothing but contempt for the Anglos who were broken—the "white boys." The "woods" refuse to associate with new Anglos until those Anglos prove themselves, not against other Anglos, but against Blacks and Latinos, because when the lines are drawn on the yard, many Anglos will quake under the verbal barrage perfected by urban Blacks, or be broken by the sheer solidarity shown by the Latinos.

Compound this with the belief by many Blacks and Latinos have that all Anglos are potential punks, and you have a scenario that is ripe for bloodshed. On the one hand, you have a group of minority criminals with the ingrained idea of the necessity of standing together, and a hatred and contempt for the "Man," who is always white. On the other hand, you have a group of mostly middle-class Anglos who have bought into the image of urban Blacks and Chicanos as violent gang members.

The minorities are predisposed to break the Anglos and the Anglos are ready to be broken, because they will not stand together against all challengers. So, on many units, in the dayrooms where benches are reserved by race and willingness to fight for the privilege, Latinos may have eight benches, Blacks eight, "woods" two benches, and the "white boys" standing against the wall or sitting on the floor.

The white gangs capitalize on this. They will approach "woods" who are nonetheless being called out often, knowing the weariness and fear of constantly looking over one's shoulder will make that Anglo receptive to charges that the Blacks and Lainos will "kill you, because they're animals and we have to stick together." This racism pervades all units. I am not suggesting that the Blacks and Latinos love one another. In fact, the greatest majority of interracial rioting is between Blacks and Latinos, usually after some small group of Blacks refuses to back down when confronted with a question of disrespect by a group of maligned Latinos. In such situations, a conference will be held between the speakers of the Latino "tangos." A vote will be taken and if a riot is decided upon, all differences between them are dropped. A time and place is chosen, usually on the yard, and at the appointed time, every Latino is expected to be there, and most of them show.

The same is not true for Blacks, which is good for the Latinos, because if the Blacks coupled solidarity with their overwhelming numerical superiority, they would be impossible to overcome. The Blacks, however, seem to respond more readily to a personal threat, not a racial one. For Latinos, once a threat has been articulated as directed against Latino pride, it is all Latinos' duty to respond. However, a Latino or Black coming into the system doesn't have the day-in, day-out fears that the Anglos do: that someone will hit you from behind, in the shower, in the halls, on the runs, in the dayroom, or that a crowd will rush into your cell. The solidarity among members of the minority races keeps them safe, except from each other. The fragmentation among Anglos, plus their symbolic representation of all that the minorities hate, keeps them victims.

CHAPTER TWENTY-ONE

parole, good time, and discharge

Now, to what you've all been waiting for: the frustrating rules governing an inmate's release from prison. First—parole is not a right; it is not guaranteed to any inmate. Parole is a privilege. It is granted by the Texas Board of Pardons and Paroles, which consists of eighteen men and women who were appointed to their seats due to their avowed interest in law and order. Second—parole will be awarded when the members of the board decide, and their decision is subjective. It is also influenced by the political winds of the day, and by pressures brought to bear by overcrowded prisons and available money to build new ones. So, if a convict tells you he is "up for parole," don't rush out to buy him clothes. All he is saying is that he is now eligible and that the board will shortly review his case and consider him for parole.

Before I go into details, let me stress those two points. Parole is not guaranteed, and there is no way to predict what the board will do in any given case. A man serving a twenty-year sentence for robbery may become eligible for parole after two and one-half years and be granted parole. Then again, he could be denied, reviewed every year thereafter and denied each time until he has done his entire twenty years, and it would all be perfectly legal, although rare.

Discharge refers to one of two things. A convict who has done his entire sentence day-for-day as in the above example must be released and is under absolutely no state supervision. (Unless he is a convicted sex offender and fits certain criteria. The Legislature has recently passed some new laws concerning sex offenders, and I will address their special case at the end of this chapter.) A convict eligible for mandatory supervision must be released when his good and his flat time equal his sentence of record, unless he committed his crime on or after September of 1996. For those inmates, the parole board has the authority, under something called Discretionary Mandatory Discharge, to block mandatory discharge on a "case-by-case basis if it determines that an inmate's good conduct record does not accurately reflect the potential for rehabilitation and that the offender's release would endanger the public." Inmates released under mandatory supervision are under most of the restrictions faced by an inmate granted parole. Many convicts are not eligible for mandatory supervision.

Both parole eligibility and date of discharge are determined by three factors: 1) the date one's crime was committed; 2) what type of crime was committed—for example: an aggravated offense is one which is so designated by the Legislature, as is a 3g offense. Both usually involve use of a weapon, or are committed against a peace officer or child, or are sexual offenses, but *any* crime can fall into this category if designated by the legislature. In any case, a man convicted of either must serve a set length of time before becoming eligible for parole and is not eligible for mandatory supervision. This means he either makes parole or does his sentence day-for-day, and good time is useless to him—and 3) an inmate's disciplinary record—which determines his good-time earning class and actual good time earned. Much of the information in this chapter was taken from *Parole in Texas,* an invaluable resource book offered by the Texas Board of Pardons and Paroles. Write them at 8610 Shoal Creek Blvd., Austin, Texas 78757, to request a copy.

Good time and Class

What is good time? Simply put, it is time, figured in days, awarded for being "good" enough to be promoted to a certain good-time earning class. For those inmates not serving aggravated sentences, or those serving non-3g offenses, good time determines parole eligibility and discharge dates. How? Imagine an inmate is awarded one day for every day he serves—called "30 for 30." Let's say he is serving a twenty-year sentence and draws 30 for 30 from the moment his sentence starts and he does not *lose* good time. If eligible for mandatory supervision, he *must* be released in ten years. This is a hypothetical example. Inmates may receive less good time or more good time, as Appendix F shows.

Inmates are eligible for parole when their good time plus flat time equals either one-third or one-fourth of their sentence, unless they are serving aggravated sentences or were convicted of 3g offenses. (Inmates not in the latter two categories convicted before 1987 mostly fall into the one-third bracket; since 1987, most fall into the one-fourth bracket.)

So, that same hypothetical convict doing a twenty-year sentence, drawing 30 for 30, will serve either two and one-half years before parole eligibility, (one-fourth of twenty being five years, and the state awarded him two and one-half years,) or will serve three years and four months, (one-third of twenty years being eighty months, and the state gave him forty, meaning he must serve forty.)

What is *class*? If you remember, in the introduction I mentioned three concepts you needed to understand: custody, status and class. The first two are essentially the same—when one talks of status, one is talking of minimum, medium, or close custody designations, which determine the privileges one is allowed. Class is closely aligned to this. Class, like custody, can be upgraded or downgraded, depending on the inmate's disciplinary record. There are two major groups of good-time earning classes, each broken into smaller groups. They are, in descending order of good-time earning potential, State Approved Trusty (SAT) I, SAT II, SAT III, SAT IV, Line Class I, Line Class II, and Line Class III.

Newly arrived inmates are generally placed into Line Class I. Depending on their behavior, they will be promoted or demoted and accordingly draw more or less good time. The amount of good time awarded to inmates in each class is determined by the Legislature, not by TDCJ. There have been many changes, most triggered by *Ruiz v. Estelle* and its provisions mandating an end to overcrowding in Texas prisons. So, depending on when the inmate committed his crime, he will be awarded the good time that is designated in Appendix F.

As the table shows, inmates convicted before 1987 are eligible to draw what is called two for one, or "60 for 30"—the flat thirty they serve, plus the sixty days of good time. These inmates can discharge a sentence, in theory, in one-third of actual length of sentence.

In theory, of course. Good time is awarded in such a bewildering fashion that it is impossible to figure out how much is being awarded, from when and in what increments. A convict must generally rely on the TDCJ Board of Classification and its figures, and on the parole board's reckoning of an initial review date.

The reasons for this are many. First, good time, until 1995, could be backdated to date of incarceration. In other words, when an inmate is promoted from Line I to SAT IV, he can either start drawing the extra good time from that date, or it can be backdated, meaning he would be awarded whatever good time SAT IV inmates are being awarded for every day of his sentence, even though he was not in TDCJ and not in that class. Many inmates, prior to 1995, through the good graces of supervisors or higher-ranking TDCJ security, had their good time backdated. Another way this worked was that if an inmate was demoted, say from SAT II to Line Class I, when and if he was promoted, the Board of Classification could decide to backdate his good time and award him for the year or two he didn't draw SAT II good time.

Second, what may also happen is that every promotion (and demotion) must be approved by the Board of Classification. So, if the unit board promotes me and forwards the recommendation to the state board, I do not know when the state board approves my promotion or when I will start drawing the extra good time, and I don't know how to refigure my parole eligibility date.

Third, any good time lost due to disciplinary action cannot be regained. This means that if an inmate has accumulated ten years of good time and has a discharge date within two years, if he receives a Level I disciplinary case and loses all his good time, it is gone forever. He has in essence been sentenced to at least another five years (the five it will take him to accumulate five years of good time at 30 for 30), especially if he is also demoted to a class that draws less good time.

However, once he becomes eligible for parole, good time does not come into play again unless he is eligible for mandatory supervision.

Once he is eligible for parole, the board will do one of three things—it can grant parole; deny parole and schedule another date for review, (called a set-off) in one, two or three years; or, if he is within three years of discharge, it can give him a serve-all.

The parole board gives many reasons for set-offs or serve-alls, many of which seem to lack logic. Recently, there have been some rumblings from elected officials that parole board members are simply denying parole without actually reviewing anyone. Some legislators have proposed doing away with parole totally, which may well happen in the not-too-distant future. However, for that to happen, new laws would have to be written to conform more closely to what is called "truth-in-sentencing." Under this concept, a man sentenced to twenty years actually does twenty years. Under truth-in-sentencing, courts would be limited to shorter sentences, although inmates would actually serve more time.

As I mentioned, the parole board is a captive of politics. If the prisons have room, unlike the 1970s and early 1980s, the board will deny most convicts parole until overcrowding forces a siphoning of convicts who seem to pose the least risk of violence. Since the process of deciding when an inmate is eligible for parole is so complicated, you need to rely on the parole board's figures. There are three dates you need to remember.

If an inmate has a conviction from a crime committed prior to *August 31, 1987,* the most he will have to serve before parole eligibility is twenty years, *if* he was convicted of an aggravated crime or any offense with an affirmative finding of a deadly weapon. Any inmate convicted before that date, regardless of offense, is also eligible for mandatory supervision.

On *September 1, 1987,* the 70th Legislature created the so-called 3g offenses, which at the time were Capital Murder, Aggravated Kidnapping, Aggravated Sexual Assault, Aggravated Robbery, and any offense with an affirmative finding of a weapon. An inmate committing any crime between that date and *August 31, 1989* can do no more than fifteen years before reaching parole eligibility, but if convicted of the 3g offenses and a few others he is not eligible for mandatory supervision.

Since *September 1, 1991,* an inmate convicted of a 3g offense or other selected offenses may have to serve up to thirty-five flat years before becoming eligible for parole, and, of course, he is not eligible for mandatory supervision.

So, again, what you need to know to be sure when your friend or relative is eligible for parole is his date of conviction and whether or not his sentence is aggravated or a 3g offense. Sadly, there are many lawyers who do not tell their clients the truth and lie to them about when they will be eligible for parole. They will say, "Take the fifteen (or twenty or thirty), because you will be eligible in three and get out in five." There is no way possible to tell, before eligibility is actually figured, when an inmate will become eligible, much less receive parole. The best way to be certain of an inmate's parole eligibility is to call the board, provide them with the inmate's name and TDCJ number and ask that you be provided with that inmate's eligibility date.

What can *you* do to assist him in making parole? You can encourage him to follow all rules and to pursue his education, of course. (More on this topic in Chapter 24.) But more specifically, you can encourage him to create a *parole packet*, which will include the following:

1. Names, addresses, and phone numbers of relatives who are offering the inmate a place to stay. Do not limit the list to just names and addresses—be specific. Say, "Jane Doe, my aunt, lives at 1234 Somesuch Street in Dallas. This is a three-bedroom home, and also living with my aunt are her seventeen-year-old daughter, and my Uncle, John, who has his own plumbing company, John's Reliable Plumbing, telephone, (555) 222-2222. My aunt volunteers at Calvary First Church, is active in the PTA and can be reached at (555) 222-2222." The board seeks information on which to make its decisions—the more detailed and specific you are, the better.
2. Names, addresses, and phone numbers of people or corporations offering the inmate employment. Letters from them are also important.
3. A written history of the inmate's prior employment.
4. A written history of the inmate's educational achievements, both in the free-world and in prison. Include certificates and copies of diplomas.

5. The inmate's legal history, including both juvenile and adult crimes, and prison disciplinary history. Yes, the board likely has a copy of all this, but including it allows an inmate to address his history and include remorse and justification or mitigation.

6. A written goal statement, outlining immediate goals, six-month goals, first-year goals and long-term goals, which allow the board to see that inmates actually plan for the future and allows them to discern the believability of that planning. Include educational, occupational, and personal goals.

7. Letters from every person who can attest to the inmate's positive qualities. These letters need not say, "I believe the board should release Inmate Jones." They can simply say, "I believe Inmate Jones is a good person and displays good work habits and has always exhibited a good attitude." Supply anything that might convince the board that this inmate has positive qualities and has the backing of his friends, family, and community should be included.

You should put the package together with the inmate's help and mail it to the parole board at least one year before he is eligible for review. Update it constantly. Add to it. If and when the inmate receives a set-off, write more letters. Express your disappointment with the decision, and say that while you understand their reasons, you want to reiterate your support for that inmate.

There are people who will encourage you to hire a parole lawyer. I am not one of them. Parole lawyers will do essentially what I am recommending that you and the inmate do—talk to potential employers, collect personal information, and package it in a precise, readable package. You can do the same thing, and it will provide a focus for strengthening your relationship with the inmate. However, if you know that neither you nor the inmate possesses the skills, time, or initiative to put the packet together, and you can afford the attorney, go ahead, because the package is essential. But parole packets should and can be compiled by inmates and their families, and the money given to attorneys better spent on educational opportunities for the inmate or in giving him a stake for when he is released.

Sex Offenders

In 1999, the legislature increased the registration requirements of sex offenders. In addition, there is a law whereby any person convicted of certain sexual offenses and serving prison time is liable to face civil commitment. The process for this is initiated by TDCJ officials, who are required to identify those sex offenders—even though they may have completed every day of their sentence—who now face the possibility of having to face another trial and further commitment. This law is new, and it has yet to be seen if criminals who are in fact committed will serve more time; whether they will serve that in prison, mental hospitals, or community halfway houses; or what additional strictures those offenders actually face. TDCJ is proceeding very cautiously in this area. If anyone you know has been convicted of rape, sexual assault, or indecency with a child, you should be aware that he or she faces the possibility of civil commitment. In addition, there are a number of bewildering registration requirements with which you and they need to become familiar.

CHAPTER TWENTY-TWO

what to do in emergencies

*T*his topic was the birthing idea for this book. In January of 1993, my brother fell ill and my family was not only unsure how to contact me— they did not know the procedure to follow so that I might attend his funeral after he died. This hurt my family and myself deeply, that I could not be there to receive and give comfort. The Texas prison system places many conditions on this type of furlough, but it is allowed. But in such a situation, time is of the essence. If you want to get your relative out in time to see his dying mother, or to attend a memorial service for his daughter, then you *must* follow TDCJ guidelines, especially the guidelines that specify the people authorized to contact TDCJ with the details of a situation.

For TDCJ officials, this is an issue loaded with problems. Most state officials are sincerely sorry when tragedy befalls the family members of convicts and they do not want to seem heartless. However, security is a priority, and the system cannot allow just anyone to call and say, "John Doe's mom is dying, can you let him come and see her? She's his only relative." While his mother may in fact be dying, and while she may in fact be his only relative, the state must have the paperwork to document her illness from a reputable physician in case the inmate is furloughed and something goes wrong during the furlough. He can commit a crime, try to escape, get into a violent episode during the ceremony, or be involved in any of a number of incidents that will reflect poorly on everyone involved.

So, if a member of your family is ill and you want to get word to an inmate, by all means contact the unit chaplain. He will talk to the inmate, counsel him, and do whatever he can to ready the inmate for the emotional process of dealing with grief and anger, if death is a result.

However, if a family member is mortally ill or dies, the process is different, and should *not* be handled directly by you, especially if you desire your relative to be granted a furlough to attend a memorial service or funeral.

If a Relative is Dying

TDCJ defines relatives as parents, spouse, siblings, half-siblings, children, and surrogate parents who have been so claimed and are so recorded in TDCJ files. In this case, you need to have the handling physician, via written communication, contact prison officials. When I say written communication, I mean:

1. by letter, which may be too slow, but must be addressed to:
   Bureau of Classification and Records
   Post Office Box 99
   Huntsville, TX; 77342-0099
2. by Fax, to 409-294-6227
3. by telegram, through Western Union to:
   EASYLINK 620-759-75;TDCJ-ID; Huntsville, TX.

The physician needs to include in his communication:

1. the inmate's name and TDCJ number
2. the name and location of the hospital, hospice, nursing home, or private home where the patient is located
3. the nature and seriousness of the illness
4. the physician's certification of the patient's critical illness
5. the telephone number and fax number of the attending physician

Do not deviate from this. *Do not* think that you can call the warden and chaplain and somehow take a shortcut. If you do that, you will waste time, because the chaplain and warden will tell you to do exactly what I am telling you to do. This is TDCJ policy, and TDCJ officials will follow it.

If a Relative has Died

Again, what is called for is written communication, but this time from the funeral home director. In this case, you will be requesting that the inmate be allowed to attend some type of service. The director needs to send the following information:

1. the inmate's name and TDCJ number
2. the deceased person's name and relation to the inmate
3. the date, time and location of the service
4. the full name of the funeral home director, the business name of the funeral home, its address, the telephone and fax numbers of the director

Your purpose in all this is to convince TDCJ to grant the inmate an emergency furlough to visit with his dying relative or attend a memorial service. You should realize that the system does not like to grant those furloughs. In fact, it has a set of criteria that will automatically disqualify most inmates.

The inmate must be:

1. at least line class I
2. within twelve months of parole eligibility
3. not have a pending or unresolved felony or immigration detainer
4. have been in TDCJ for at least six months
5. not be in TDCJ for: homicide (capital murder, voluntary manslaughter, or other homicide), kidnapping, any sexual assault, any robbery; assault (aggravated, injury to a child or an elderly person, or other assault), or any offense in which the inmate used or exhibited a deadly weapon
6. have had a clear disciplinary record for the prior six months
7. not have a record of assaults on prison staff

TDCJ makes the determination to grant emergency furloughs on a case-by-case basis, depending on the inmate's status; length of time incarcerated; the distance to be traveled; the location of the service and proximity to TDCJ units; and availability of staff. There is a long-standing rumor that TDCJ will be swayed by the willingness of family to pay the costs of transportation, including the few days' salary of any law enforcement of any officers involved. I don't know if this is true. However, I don't think it would hurt if you contacted the local sheriff's office and offered to help pay the expenses of any deputies detailed to escort the inmate and guard him.

If an Inmate Dies

There is a topic closely related to the death of a relative of an inmate—if your inmate relative contracts a mortal disease or dies in prison, then how are you notified? TDCJ will go to its records and notify the person whom the inmate has indicated he wants notified in case of an emergency. If that person is unavailable, TDCJ will go down its list of that inmate's relatives. If an inmate dies, TDCJ officials will notify you and will notify the county coroner to come and view the inmate, but they will not order an autopsy short of extraordinary circumstances.

If an inmate is determined to be dying, there is a chance that the parole board will grant that inmate a special-needs parole. If that is a possibility in your case, you should contact the parole board in Austin, because every case is different, depending on the length of time the inmate is expected to live, whether he is ambulatory, and other criteria.

How many of you can remember living in a dormitory like this? If you can, you're old enough to remember prison conditions that were later declared unconstitutional by Ruiz. For more on this, turn to Page 5.

The **Texas Prison News** **ECHO**

Inside this edition...	
Letters to editor	Pg. 2
Dispatches	Pg. 3
Dear Darby	Pg. 3
Chef Brown presents	Pg. 3
Chris' Tahitian Tune	
The courts and	Pg. 4
administrative segregation	
RUIZ: Overcrowding	Pg. 6
College graduates	Pg. 6-7
Unit activities	Pg. 8
It's your health	Pg. 9
Legal news	Pg. 11
CJ news briefs	Pg. 11
Commentaries	Pg. 12

Texas civil commitment law unlike those in other states. See why...

(Please turn to Page 10)

Published Continuously Since 1928   Volume 72, No. 9 — September 2000   Distributed Free to Texas Prisoners

–Administrative segregation units multiply despite history's warnings–

Controlling the mind and body

In 1984, the population in the then-Texas Department of Corrections was approximately 35,000 inmates, with 1,102 of them in safekeeping or administrative segregation. While the overall Texas prison population has almost quintupled since that time, the number of inmates in ad/seg has risen eightfold during the same period. The concept of management by isolation has caught on in American prisons and will not go away soon. In the next three editions, The ECHO will examine this concept and the issues associated with it. We begin with a short look at the history of ad/seg and at some relevant court decisions.

BY JORGE ANTONIO RENAUD

Ever since there have been laws to break, men and women have broken them and been judged for their crimes. Throughout history, lords and barons kept their cellars full of local criminals and debtors, but for centuries those makeshift jails were mainly holding pens, layovers until the accused were found not guilty (rare) or hanged (more likely.) Things must have changed by the 3rd century, because the Roman judge Ulpian, recording his disgust, lamented, "provincial governors usually sentence people to be held in prison or to be fettered. This is illegal, since such forms of punishment have been prohibited. . . Prison ought to be used for detention only, not for punishment."

FIRST IN A SERIES

The idea of prison as punishment didn't fully catch on until 1275, when the Statutes of Westminster ordered rapists to serve two years in prison. Three hundred and twenty years later, the British lord treasurer ordered prisons built for two reasons, "the one for safe custody, the other for correction."

A look inside the Auburn, New York prison, built during the 19th century. Extreme solitary confinement conditions contributed to a high rate of insanity among its prisoners. (Photo courtesy Cayuga County Historian)

Reflecting class divisions, prisons often were repositories of men and women out of favor with the local powers, and conditions were undeniably terrible.

Modern penology tries to occupy a higher moral ground. Prison reformers have tried to eradicate the stink of prisons past by insisting on educational, vocational and recreational programs. One facet of prison that has rarely changed, however, is the existence of solitary confinement. The moldy castle basements of medieval Europe, the frigid gulags of Siberian Russia, the xi nao (brainwashing) camps of China: all resorted to one proven method of control – the isolation of troublesome prisoners.

It is difficult, if not impossible, to accurately document what goes on in prisons

whose mission is the long-term segregation of convicts. Prisoners accuse, administrators deny; convicts exaggerate, correctional officers stonewall. To see through the smoke, it is necessary to study the origin of control units in this country and to then examine those units under the light cast by two groups – the academic observers that document their effects and the courts that allow them life.

American penal philosophy has three roots, the first two of Quaker origin – the Pennsylvania system and the Auburn model. The Pennsylvania system, founded in 1790, relied on religious instruction, corporal punishment and the complete isolation of prisoners, to better allow them to meditate upon their sins. Labor was restricted to handicrafts that were done in-cell and for which the prisoners were paid.

In the Auburn model of the 1820s, prisoners were permitted to work together, thus allowing more production. Not surprisingly, this model found much favor with capitalist American prison administrators, who were forever looking for ways to keep costs down and, in some cases, to pad their pockets. The Auburn model also prohibited all communication between convicts. Both

The moldy castle basements of medieval Europe, the frigid gulags of Siberian Russia, the xi nao (brainwashing) camps of China: all resorted to one proven method of control – the isolation of troublesome prisoners.

See SEG, Page 4

Criminal justice news briefs...

Roy Criner released after Gov. Bush signs pardon

Montgomery County District Attorney Michael McDougal recently joined State District Judge Mike Mayes and Montgomery County Sheriff Guy Williams in calling for a pardon freeing Roy Criner, a state prisoner convicted a decade ago of rape.

New DNA evidence, along with new witnesses brought forward by Criner's family, convinced McDougal, Mayes and Williams to sign a request to the Texas Board of Pardons and Paroles for the pardon.

On Monday, August 14, the Texas Board of Pardons and Paroles voted to make a recommendation to Gov. George W. Bush that he pardon Criner.

Bush signed the pardon on August 15, allowing Criner to walk out of the Montgomery County Jail Tuesday afternoon, a free man for the first time in over ten years.

Criner was convicted in the 1990 aggravated sexual assault of 16-year-old Deanna Ogg. The girl's bludgeoned body was found in east Montgomery County. She had been stabbed 11 times.

Criner, originally charged with murder, was convicted of the sexual assault charge after the murder charge was dropped due to insufficient evidence.

The new DNA evidence showed that the Criner was not the person who committed the rape and murder according to McDougal, who previously contended that Criner could have used a condom when he raped the girl.

The Texas Court of Criminal Appeals has twice ruled against Criner, overturning lower court rulings in his favor. Mayes ruled in January 1998 that Criner was entitled to a new trial because DNA testing showed that semen found on the victim was not his. The Court of Criminal Appeals, in a 6-3 ruling, again overturned the ruling, citing McDougal's argument that Criner could have worn a condom.

Since 1997, the governor has pardoned three state prisoners convicted of rape or sexual assault based on new DNA evidence ruling them out as suspects.

DNA fails to clear Ricky McGinn

A DNA analysis of crime scene evidence taken in the 1993 rape and murder of 12-year-old Stephanie Flanary, failed to clear death row inmate Ricky McGinn of the crime.

McGinn, who was given a stay of execution by Gov. George W. Bush minutes before his scheduled June execution made national headlines because of the Bush presidential campaign and growing concerns over the excessive use of the death penalty in Texas.

McGinn's execution has been rescheduled for September.

See CJ BRIEFS, Page 11

Segregation: malevolence kept at bay?

BY JORGE ANTONIO RENAUD

Prison is, ultimately, about prevention. It is not about rehabilitation – we do not know what, if anything, is "wrong," so we cannot ever say it has been "fixed." It is not about punishment – the psychology of individuals is so different that what hurts one may give twisted pleasure to another and encourage the behavior we are trying to eradicate.

The purpose behind locking a person away for an act is to prevent that person from committing that act for a period of time. But even in a controlled environment, certain individuals are so dangerous that

they must be kept separate, because the most that any prison can do is protect those who live and work there from the violent inclinations of a terrible few.

COMMENTARY

Separation and protection, in a nutshell, are what administrative segregation is all about. The protection of the rules-abiding inmate majority; the protection of staff; the efficient management of educational and vocational programs, all argue for the existence of administrative segregation.

But what happens if the criteria for separation – and for a return to the general population – are so secret or ambiguous that assignment to ad/seg is used to punish the merely nonconforming? What happens when mentally ill inmates, frustrated at their inability to understand the rules or to communicate in a coherent fashion, are assigned to ad/seg, where their illness deepens into psychosis and dementia? What happens if the prospect of another feces-splattered day is too much for a correctional officer who has been, to that point, a well-meaning

See COMMENTARY, Page 4

CHAPTER TWENTY-THREE

the echo

*T*he *Echo* is the Texas Prison Newspaper—our newspaper. It is tabloid-sized and published every month or two, then distributed via truck mail to the units and then to the living quarters. The *Echo* has been published more or less continuously since 1928 and has a circulation of 100,000 or so, giving it some standing among Texas papers.

The *Echo*'s contents can be divided into three types of articles: reprints of penal-related stores written for other papers; occasional columns or editorials written by the *Echo*'s staff; and recognition-type pieces: graduation notices, results of sports tournaments, and similar short articles submitted by inmates.

There is a Letters to the Editor page, and an advice column written by a mystery convict. This columnist, who like Madonna and Elvis has reached first-name status—Dear Darby—offers sarcastic and hilarious advice to letters that are genuine but often sound made-up. His column is a tradition and undoubtedly the most-read part of any given issue.

The *Echo* is censored and will not print letters or articles that are overly critical of the prison system in general or its officials in particular. While it may use an article that condemns the death penalty, it will almost never criticize the current Texas governor, the parole board or the system director and his policies, all of which very likely have a direct effect on prison policies and how they are implemented in Texas prisons.

The *Echo* prints quite a bit of poetry and fiction written by Texas inmates. While you may not associate poetry with a newspaper, inmates will scan the creativity section for verses to inscribe on cards to their loved ones, thus adding personality to their mail. The *Echo*'s pages are also a proving ground for any young or unpublished poets who are hesitant to test the outside publications until gauging reaction.

The system uses the *Echo* to disseminate information or legal notices it wants all Texas convicts to be aware of. By this, I mean that if a federal court issues a ruling directly affecting Texas prisons, or if TDCJ is amending a broad rule or policy, it will publish the order or rule in the *Echo* as a way of notifying all inmates.

However, this assumes that all Texas inmates get a copy of each *Echo*, and that isn't so. Usually, the *Echo* arrives at a unit's law library or schoolhouse, and the issues are distributed to living areas. A certain number may be placed in each dayroom, and eventually most minimum custody inmates will have access to each issue. But inmates in close custody or in ad/seg are at the mercy of unit policy or individual officers. Some units require ad/seg inmates and close custody inmates to request a copy of each *Echo*, in writing, and then will make only half-hearted attempt to fulfill each request.

Regardless of its censored, repetitive nature, most Texas convicts look forward to the *Echo*. They scan its pages for mention of themselves or friends in the recognition pages. They read the articles, reprints or not, for indication of coming legislation that may affect their eligibility or actual chances for parole.

They laugh at Darby, complain at the lack of meaty editorials, and every now and then are directly influenced by information or encouragement found in the *Echo*'s pages. It is, truly, their paper.

Not only can you receive the *Echo*; you can submit articles. If you want to receive it, yearly subscriptions are twelve dollars. Mail a money order or personal check to: the *Echo*, P.O Box 99; Huntsville, TX 77342-0099. Any article or information you wish to submit should be sent to the same address. One final thing—you won't find articles about riots or lockdowns or anything even remotely resembling breaking news in the *Echo*. The officials in charge of publishing the paper insist that the *Echo* focus on the "positive" aspects of prison. If you remember that, you won't be disappointed.

CHAPTER TWENTY-FOUR

helping ex-cons stay out of prison

Why do we kill, or rob, or sell drugs, or write hot checks, or beat up strangers, or abuse and rape women and children? Why are we criminals? Is it because we are poor? Because we were abused ourselves? Because our friends do it? Do our criminal actions arise from need, rage, despair, or simple greed?

I don't know if anyone can answer these questions. However, once someone is convicted and comes to prison, that person is identified in a way and molded into something he wasn't before. The guy on the corner who we suspected was "up to no good" is now a full-fledged convict, and a convict trying to stay out after release from prison will face a different set of problems than a young person who is just now breaking the law and has yet to go to prison.

I have no insights to offer those who wish to keep people out of trouble and out of jail. If you are reading this, it is probably too late for that, anyway. What I have to offer is hope—that with your help, your loved one in prison can, upon release, defy the odds and stay out. This may sound strange; hope, and suggestions on how to stay free from a man in for the third time, in the face of cold statistics that show almost sixty percent of all convicts returning to prison.

However, when I first thought of writing this book, I suspected something—few friends and relatives of convicts have clear concepts of prison, and thus do not know how to help convicts, except to send money and to visit occasionally. And if there is one thing my time in prison has taught me, it is this: prison changes everyone who comes into contact with it. It perverts values, attitudes, and morality. The rage, fear, violence, despair, and hopelessness that permeate every prison in the world make prisoners assume postures and don masks in order to cope. But those postures and masks run contrary to the honesty and forthright nature expected of free-world citizens. And, *if a convict's friends and relatives do not realize this,* they will not know how to help the convict combat the effects of prison. And once on the streets again, it is too late.

I believe that if a convict's relatives and friends are aware of and help a convict address his psychological, educational, and emotional deficiencies while he is still in prison, that convict stands a better chance of staying out than the convict whose relatives know little of what he has experienced and have not helped him prepare for release. Because, if not addressed early, youthful habits that brought one to prison will harden into adult patterns that cannot be shed, like so much useless skin, once one is at the release gate.

So, this chapter will be a little more suggestive than factual. I will give you a few concrete dos and don'ts, but more than anything, I will try to help you understand the importance of addressing those three areas convicts are demonstrably deficient in. They may overlap, and what I say of one may echo in another, but understanding how you can help us strengthen ourselves is key to our staying out.

Psychological and Emotional Needs

One reason cited by the parole board for denying parole is that an inmate has failed to adjust to institutional rules. There is a paradox here. One cannot gauge if an inmate has adjusted to institutional rules other than by his adherence to or violation of those rules as indicated by his disciplinary record. If he has a perfect disciplinary record the board will assume he has in fact adjusted to them. Now, if those rules were all fair and intended to assist him in addressing his problems; if they had logic and fairness in their intent and application; if they were impartially enforced, then a case could be made that this best interests lay in following all of them, all of the time. But the system doesn't work like that. The rules are contradictory, capricious, and designed to subjugate, dehumanize, and thus control men who have demonstrated a willingness to prey on their fellow citizens, or at least sell them an illegal bag of marijuana.

So, if he follows every rule without question, he is training himself to be an automaton, allowing poorly educated, ill-trained guards to decide every facet of his life—how to dress, when and what to eat, when and where to go to work, when and where to sleep and awaken. Every aspect of his life is controlled by another person, and every decision is left to others, rendering that inmate totally incapable of living in a free, competitive society that not only prizes but demands independence and rapid decision making.

While adjusting to institutional rules and life and following *all* rules may result in a clean disciplinary record and in the approval of the parole board and thus release, it will almost certainly result in a convict's return. Convicts understand this, if only subconsciously, because we understand that in the free world no one makes you walk in a straight line without speaking, that no one enters your home and searches your property every day—that in the free world, more often than not, you decide the small choices that govern the course of your life. We understand that prison is a perversion, a twisted version of reality, and so are the rules, and we then resist prison's rote dehumanization in one of two ways.

We learn to circumvent the rules. We learn to role-play, lie, and manipulate those with power over us. This is easy for many of us, because we were manipulative in our search of dope, money, or an easy life before coming to prison. Before, we practiced our speeches to wives, mothers, fathers, and employers. Now, we practice our talks to the parole board—we practice being remorseful. We learn what worked for others, never stopping to ask why those others *returned* to prison and are now giving us advice. We don't stop to see that lies, manipulation, and cynicism may get us around the rules but in the end those false values will hurt more than help.

There is another alternative. This is to accept that, unless we are innocent, prison is self-inflicted. It is to understand that this system is huge, does not care for our safety or rehabilitation, and in fact depends on our return for its existence. It is to believe that our primary goal should be to survive with dignity; to not react with violence unless in self-defense; to follow all rules unless they are life-threatening; to establish our own routine and to be as independent as possible; to set goals; and, most importantly, to constantly improve our minds.

Sadly, this route is harder than the first. Having been judged failures by society and by our family, it is all too easy for convicts to see ourselves only as failures. We become defensive and adopt an us-vs-them attitude, and the only people whose opinion matters is *ours*. The approval of our peers is the motivating force in our life, and to most of our peers, a real man curses the guards, a real man riots when his homeboys do, and a real man reacts with fury and violence when someone shows him the slightest disrespect.

This attitude twists our morality and values into something totally different from what is expected from a citizen in the free world. Since the romanticism of the outlaw is preferable to the stigma of the outcast, we glorify our status as rebels and view with contempt the staid, humdrum lives of the conforming, common people. Yet, we secretly desire that humdrum life.

Few inmates have the strength to combat either the institutionalization of prison or the coarsening of values caused by conformity to peer pressure. How can you help?

First, you must constantly reassure the inmate that while what he did was wrong, it does not define him in your eyes. This is crucial. You may feel that you must feed him little white lies, and that you must tell him that you are not ashamed of him and of his crime. But that isn't true, and he knows it and will resent your condescending attitude. You must be truthful but aware of his vulnerability. You can say, "Yes, I was angry. And yes, I was ashamed when so-and-so called me and rubbed in the fact that my son was in prison. Yes, I was hurt. But I love you. You can overcome this and my love for you will not depend on you not getting cases here or on making parole, and my love for you means I am willing to help you if you are willing to help yourself."

You must strive to keep him a part of your life. One of the worst pieces of advice that TDCJ gives to relatives of convicts is that they shouldn't tell inmates when someone dies, or when someone close to them is very sick, or when their wife has obviously taken up with another man, or when some other tragedy befalls someone close to that inmate.

TDCJ does not advise that out of a concern for the inmate or his family, but to maintain the security of the system. If you lie to a convict, or do not tell him when something tragic happens to someone he cares about, not only does he still have to process that anger or grief, but he will have to deal with the anger and resentment toward you for hiding it from him, and at the implied belief that he is too irresponsible to be told such news, or worse—that he is too unworthy to be included in the family network.

You must continue to make an inmate part of your life. There are easy ways to do this. You can buy ten postcards, stamp them, and put them in your purse or in the glove compartment of your car. When you go to a new restaurant, scribble a few lines that describe the meal or music or the waiter's snobby attitude. When you leave a movie, and it made you especially happy or sad, or excited, tell him why in a short sentence. If you hear a corny joke he'd like, write it on a postcard and mail it. Mail a couple of postcards a week, and an occasional longer, more in-depth letter every month or so. Send him photos, newspaper clippings of local happenings, news of his friends—good news or bad. Keep the free world, with its possibilities and realities, fresh in his mind.

You see, as the months become years, the letters tend to become more seasonal, more dutiful. Inmates begin to feel that they are not a part of the family. To fill that void, they will make associations with other inmates, many of which are detrimental. They will feel that the inmates are their family, and their expectations will be the ones that matter.

Don't make promises you can't keep. If you fail to do something that you've promised, address the situation. There is nothing more frustrating to an inmate than having someone promise to make a call to an attorney, or promise to mail a needed research book, or promise to do something that matters deeply to that inmate and then it doesn't happen, and when he asks why, he is ignored. Don't let your guilt or procrastination worsen the relationship between you. He is already ashamed of being an adult in prison, unable to provide for his family, still asking mother for money and favors, and being placed in the position of having to repeatedly ask about something that was promised to him only increases his guilt and frustration. It is not the fact that the promised thing was not forthcoming—that can be dealt with. It is the fact that you did not bother to tell him so he could make other arrangements, and what that says to him about how you respect his wishes and needs. Believe me—he will understand your having to pay bills, or losing your checkbook, or just forgetting, but you have to say so. Don't let the situation deteriorate.

These things are important. They don't take much extra time. They may not seem important to you, but believe me—going that extra mile and making that extra effort to keep the inmate believing that he is loved and in your thoughts will do wonders for his attitude, and it may be the difference between him joining a gang and deciding his family deserves better than that.

Educational Needs

When I say education, I don't mean the pursuit of a degree or a specific vocational trade. While those things are worthy of pursuit, the prison environment makes it difficult to attain those particular goals. A chance encounter with a spiteful guard could result in an inmate being tossed from vocational school, and if he had all his eggs in that basket, he would be overly devastated. Or, if he must wait until he is shipped to a unit that offers the course or college he wants, he may lose his desire, or worse, his status and custody, and fall even further behind.

Long-term specific goals, such as graduation from college, obtaining a GED, or finishing a vocational course should certainly be encouraged, but non-specific education should be a priority. The inmate should be encouraged to read and study and write—anything that will improve his self-discipline, build steady habits and, above all, give him something to focus on other than the domino tables, the recreation yards, and the gangs.

How do you do this? Mail him books and get him magazine subscriptions. Has he mentioned an interest in automobile history? Get him a subscription to *Car and Driver*. Find a few good books, maybe heavy on illustration, or with intense graphics, and mail them to him. Does he not know the history of his ethnic group? Send him biographies of Malcolm X or César Chávez, or narratives of the Irish kings, or the Peruvian natives. Pinpoint his interests. Does he speak about war? Get him one of the *Time-Life* series on World War II, or the Vietnam War, and have it mailed to him, a book at a time.

Be honest about his intellectual capabilities. If you know he has trouble with concepts, find books that do not demand much analysis. But push him, constantly, and ask him about the books you've sent, if he enjoyed them, and if he is ready for more. He may ask for *Playboy, Penthouse,* or similar magazines. Tell him you will subscribe to those if he will show you concrete proof that he is in some way advancing his intellect. Offer to enroll him in a study-by-mail course in art, or philosophy, or something he is interested in.

If he has graduated, mail him catalogues of local colleges. Find out what their entrance requirements are and mail him books so he can prepare for the tests or for the basic courses. Many colleges will be more than happy to direct you to a bookstore that will sell books on how to prepare for the tests that those schools will demand for admittance. Challenge him to keep learning. Send him books on chess or magazines that contain puzzles. Surprise him with a few books by his favorite author.

Simply put—do not allow his mind to stagnate. Bitterness, despair, and the hopeless violence that follows must be kept at bay, and this is best done if a convict is made aware of this intelligence and capabilities.

After an Inmate's Release

Most men in prison have a history of failed relationships. Many have been divorced several times. Some alienated their families. Whatever the cause—drug-related theft from family members, ignoring the welfare of their wives and children—many, if not most of us, either are now or have been recently on uneasy terms with our loved ones.

It is foolhardy to believe that a man who had problems maintaining close relationships before he went to prison has somehow learned the social skills he was lacking; patience, empathy, responsibility, and the ability to communicate honestly. Although a convict may have accepted the fact that he was at fault for rupturing his family, that acceptance is not the same as possessing the skills to ensure he doesn't do it again. Those skills must be learned and honed through practice.

Most convicts are emotional cripples. They have built shells around themselves, behind which they hide their fears. They have learned to display only anger and a false joviality, a nothing-can-touch-me façade. A convict released into the free world may be incapable of establishing and maintaining close, honest relationships. If he attempts to do so and the relationship fails, that failure may well send him into a spiral of despair that will lead to behavior that will return him to prison. You need to recognize this pattern and to avoid initiating it by not asking him to intervene in family quarrels and by helping him if he seems to be in a dangerous relationship.

Let me give you a few examples of situations a convict may face that could be dangerous.

> Twenty-six-year-old Ted has been in prison since he was seventeen. He is in excellent physical condition and has attained a two-year degree. He is released and enrolls at a four-year university. He begins to interact with, and is attracted to, educated, intelligent, mature women. However, he has virtually no experience with women. His only involvements were with high-school girls, almost ten years ago. He has spent nine years fantasizing about an ideal romance, and he is all too ready to fall in love with the first woman who pays him any attention. He takes every slight to heart, and what may be a simple disagreement to her is enough to send him into despair. When she tires of his nakedly emotional neediness and decides to move on, he lashes out at her, drowns his sorrow in drugs or alcohol, or turns to his old friends, whom he knows will accept him. Either response is likely to result in his parole being violated.

> Joe gets out of prison. He is thirty, and his twenty-one-year-old niece is the light of his life. She visited him regularly, mailed him money, and kept him going. She is having problems with her boyfriend and asks Joe to speak with him. The boyfriend is young, looking for a reputation, and will likely resent Joe's intrusion. Joe hopes he can walk away if the boyfriend gets insulting, but knows that my not be possible. He doesn't know how to say no to his niece.

Assad is an ex-crack addict. He has been in prison twice, and he stole from his family to support his habit. They have reached an uneasy truce. Assad has attended NA/AA while in prison, has accepted the tenets of twelve-step recovery and immediately finds a job after release and continues attending NA/AA meetings. His family, however, looks for behavior they believe will indicate he has returned to drugs. When they believe they have found it, one of his sisters calls his employer and tells him Assad cannot be trusted. An uncle accuses Assad of stealing thirty dollars the uncle has lost. Whether or not Assad is doing drugs, the mistrust and suspicion he faces, and his inability to deal with the pain and anger that these accusations cause him, makes him say, "So what? I may as well be who they think I am."

Thirty-four-year-old Betty was visited frequently by her mother during her five-year incarceration. Betty's sister, Martha, resents the money their mother "wasted" on trips to see Betty, thinking the money would have been better spent on Martha's children. When Betty is released, this animosity threatens to spill over into other areas of Betty's life. She feels her sister's resentment, and the anger that is part of the children's attitude toward her is unbearable.

These problems exist in many situations, not just the families of ex-convicts. But the truth is that when placed under pressure, most of us revert to past behavior, and for ex-convicts, those ways were violent or self-destructive. Reverting to them will surely result in a return to prison and to additional pain and despair for their families, often turning those who didn't support the convict against those who did. Convicts simply don't have a reservoir of experience to draw upon, and they must be given the time to build that experience.

So what can you do? You can't totally shield someone from all family quarrels. You can, however, recognize that an ex-convict should not be thrust into situations where the outcome will result in his being alienated from his family. He should not be asked to mediate arguments. He should be encouraged to remain neutral, and to explain to the family that he does not feel he is ready to give advice but will support whatever decision is made.

I'm not encouraging you to totally coddle him. Demand he be responsible, but only for his actions, not for the decisions of others. He has become used to superficial relationships, and the depth of the anger and resentment that can result from family disputes can devastate him. Plus, he is vulnerable in a legal way. If a resentful family member decides to retaliate by filing false charges against a parolee, just the charges may be enough to have his parole revoked.

An ex-convict takes rejection too personally. His sense of self-esteem is extremely low. He should be encouraged to date more than one woman, unless he is married, of course, and to keep his relationships casual until he has learned to separate the trivial from the serious. If he breaks up with a woman, keep him occupied with something or someone else. Don't give him time to brood.

And, if the situation in your family is such that other siblings or family members are undergoing crises that need attention—drug addictions, or abusive relationships of their own—it may be best that you discourage your convict relative from staying with you or even visiting you. His best bet may be a halfway house, not a home where the tension and imminent violence will only worsen his problems. He needs attention and discipline and love. If you cannot truthfully give him those, it is better that he be in a structured setting with professionals who will at least do no harm.

Some Last Words

If at all possible, you should visit your convict relative or friend on a regular basis. This isn't always possible. In either case, he is just another number in white cotton to the guards who run the system. You should get in the habit of calling the unit where he is assigned and asking to speak to the warden at least once a year. Introduce yourself and ask him to give you an update on your son's behavior, or on his progress in school. Tell him that you just want him to know that you love your son, that you understand that he may get into trouble, and that if he does, he will be punished. But you should make it clear that you will not allow your son to be harassed; that you will not allow him to be set up; that you will not allow him to be raped or attacked, and that if those things happen, that you will do whatever it takes to bring those at fault to justice.

Those who run the Texas prisons are not evil, just indifferent. There is an old saying that all that is necessary for injustice to flourish is for good men to do nothing. Texas prison officials care primarily for the security of their units, the safety of their staff, and their personal well-being. They must be reminded at times that the people who they guard have families, and that those families will not stand by and let their convict relatives be brutalized.

Do not think that you will worsen a situation by calling the unit and speaking with the warden. It is better, by far, to let him know that you are supportive of your relative than to let the system believe your son is alone and uncared for. They look at his visiting records, and they know who gets visits and mail, but they do not know the extent of your care and love for your relative. Only you can demonstrate that to them.

Do not ever think you are alone. There are some wonderful organizations that have existed for years to assist convicts, and recently two have been formed to assist the families of convicts. They are the Texas Inmate Families Association, (TIFA), and INFO, Inc. I have included addresses for both in the appendix. Both have chapters in many cities, and their leaders have demonstrated a willingness to contact and lobby not only TDCJ officials, but the legislative leaders who write and revise the laws that directly affect inmates and their families. By all means, get involved.

There are other organizations that are comprised of convicts, the families of convicts, or those otherwise involved in the criminal justice system. The most active of these have historically been the American Civil Liberties Union (ACLU), and the group Citizens United for the Rehabilitation of Errants (CURE). Please, contact any of these organizations to which you feel you can donate your time and money.

The Texas prison system is changing, and there are three things driving that change—the changes fostered by *Ruiz*; the worsening staff shortage, and the December 2000 escape of seven inmates (the Connally Seven or the Texas Seven) from the Connally Unit and their murder of a policeman. These forces are manifesting themselves in different facets of prison.

In the first, the decision by the 5th Circuit Court of Appeals to remove Judge William Wayne Justice from all oversight of the *Ruiz* accords means that many prison guards believe that those accords are no longer in effect. That is not true. Most of those accords have been codified by TDCJ and placed into effect as official policy. However, the belief by guards that *Ruiz* need no longer be adhered to means that many of them ignore the limits placed upon them by *Ruiz*. As a result inmates may have to fight the battles over and over again that were fought twenty years ago. It remains to be seen if the leadership of TDCJ—as of this writing headed by Gary Johnson, who succeeded Wayne Scott—makes it clear to the rank and file that *Ruiz* must, indeed, be followed, or if doing so is left to the inmates to enforce through court challenges.

Secondly, the staff shortage is being felt in many ways. TDCJ has steadily decreased access to "non-essential" activities, meaning that recreation, church services, craft shop access, and even the field activities have been curtailed on many units, as staff are reassigned to the blocks to watch inmates in their living quarters. So, if your relative complains that he is not being allowed to go outside, or that the choir has been cut on his unit, or that he cannot make the purse for Christmas—it could all be true and be attributed to the worsening staff shortage. How TDCJ addresses this problem will determine whether or not those services are offered, to whom and for how long.

Finally, the Connally Seven left their mark on Texas prisons, as do most high-profile escapes. It is almost impossible to explain to a non-inmate how severely security has been tightened on many units. On many, one cannot walk down the hallway until one is told; as a result, logjams build up in chow halls and in shower rooms, resulting in fights and increased tension; the trusty requirements are constantly being revised, resulting in many long-time trusties being moved into the building and out of trusty camps, and including a corresponding loss of privileges. Many long-time, trusted workers in industry are being moved into the kitchen and laundry, away from access to the tools that the media so focused upon when the Connally Seven escaped. Although these long-term convicts have never been violent while in prison, and although they may form the backbone of TDCJ industry, the perception that TDCJ was too lax in classification stung TDCJ officials, and they reacted as they usually do, by imposing blanket restrictions on all Texas inmates. The result is that any convict doing at least fifty years must serve at least ten years flat before being placed into any position of trust or responsibil-ity—they cannot be in industry, cannot serve as clerks, and those restric-tions prevent many from doing anything other than mindless, numbing drudgery in highly restrictive environments.

The political tenor of this country is drifting rightward, and it has been since the late 1970s. Many of the civil rights that were granted under the Warren Burger Supreme Court to Americans in general—and by Judge William Wayne Justice to Texas convicts in particular—are slowly being eroded.

It is likely you once looked at convicts as scum, and as deserving of whatever punishment they received. But now, having been through the system with your relative or friend, you may have come to understand that convicts are people, some worse than others, but still men and women like you and your neighbors. Any man or woman can come to prison. The rights of prisoners are the first to be taken away, because they have no voice in this country, and the despair and pain of those who have been left behind—children, wives, and parents—is often also unheard. Sup-port the civil right of convicts and their families. You may be doing some-one you love, or even yourself, a favor.

APPENDIX A
Custody Levels

The following explains what custody levels exist in TDCJ-ID (Institutional Division), and gives a brief summary of the privileges allowed at each level. For a more detailed idea of the levels and privileges, see the chapters on Money, Recreation, and Segregation.

1. Minimum out, State Approved Trusty I—Eligible for four contact visits each month. Can work outside without direct supervision except for sporadic check-ups. May be assigned to trusty camp. Maximum allowed on recreation, commissary, and property privileges.
2. Minimum out, Line I—Same as above, except that may be from Line I to SAT II.
3. Minimum out, restricted—May be from Line I to SAT II. Eligible for same privileges as above. Must have direct unarmed supervision while outside the fence and cannot live in trusty camp.
4. Minimum in—May be from Line I to SAT III. Must have direct, armed supervision if outside fence. Maximum privileges on commissary, recreation, and property. Allowed from one to three contact visits monthly, depending on SAT status.
5. Medium—Line I to SAT IV. Must live in cell, unless female. Will be generally assigned to field force. No contact visits. Allowed thirty dollars commissary spending every two weeks. Allowed four hours recreation on weekdays and five hours on weekends. May participate in educational programs.
6. Close—Line II or Line III. Must live in cell and will be assigned to field force. No contact visits. Allowed twenty dollars commissary spending every two weeks. Allowed two hours recreation daily. Must have direct supervision all times away from cell. May not participate in educational programs.
7. Administrative segregation—
   a. Security detention—Considered threat to safety of staff or inmates, or threat to order and safety of institution, as evi-

denced by repeated, serious disciplinary violations; may be threat by having been identified as disruptive group (gang) member, or considered current escape risk. Has SAT IV ceiling. No contact visits. No job assignment. No educational programs except for in-cell correspondence programs. Always chained and escorted to and from cell. Always single-celled.

   b. Protective custody—Highest degree of protection available due to threats of harm from others. Has SAT III ceiling. Contact visits allowed. No job or education except as in Security Detention. Escorted at all time. (For recreation and commissary details, see Chapter 6.)

8. Death Row—Highest degree of supervision. General visits only. Either treated as ad/seg or work capable, if work program is available. Accorded privileges in line with disciplinary record.

9. Medical status—Needs special consideration due to special medical considerations, as identified by medical personnel. Are usually assigned to units and given housing and program assignments commensurate with special need. Eligibility for privileges decided by disciplinary record.

10. Mentally retarded offender program(MROP)—Has a WAIS-R (Wechsler Adult Intelligence Scale, after David Wechsler, an intelligence test created for semi-literate individuals.) full scale IQ of seventy-three or below, or a social history indicative of mental retardation. Initially assigned to MROP-sheltered facility and designated as intellectually impaired. May be reclassified or reassigned, but recommendations of the MROP treatment staff are binding on all other personnel and govern treatment. Privileges determined by disciplinary record.

11. Physically disabled—Refers to offenders with a mobility, visual, hearing, or speech impairment. May be assigned to barrier-free facility, but the Unit Classification Committee will determine offender's housing based on classification criteria. Privileges determined by disciplinary record.

(Source: TDCJ-ID Classification Plan, Revised Nov. 1999)

Modification of the Offender Classification Plan, March 2002
The TDCJ implemented the following changes to policy regarding general population offenders :

Close (CC, PC) is now General Population Level 5 (G5P5)
   Those offenders with an escape from secure adult correction facility within the last ten years (ES), who had an escape form a secure TDCJ facility within the past five years will not be assigned to a custody less restrictive than G5.

Medium (ME, PE) is now General Population Level 4 (G4P4)
   Offenders with an Security Precaution Designator (SPD) of ES, staff assault with serious injury within the last ten years (SA), or history of taking a staff member hostage (HS) will not be assigned to custody less restrictive than G4.

Minimum In (M1P1) is now General Population Level 3 (G3P3)
   Fifty-year sentence or more who have not served the required ten years for 3G [a 3G offense is defined as—murder, capital murder, indecency with a child, aggravated kidnapping, sexual assault, aggravated sexual assault, aggravated robbery, any offense with an affirmative finding of the use of a deadly weapon, and Health and Safety chapter 481.134 (c), (d), (e), and (f).] and five years for non 3G. Offenders may not be assigned to maintenance, SSI, clerk, back dock worker, or any job where the offender is allowed access to multiple areas of the unit, and these offenders may not be housed in a dormitory located outside of the main building. Offenders with an SPD (Security Precaution Designator) removal code of NE (escape designator removed by SPDRC, escape less than ten years ago), NA (staff assault designator removed by SPDRC, assault less than ten years ago), or NS (hostage designator removed by SPDRC) will not be assigned to a custody less restrictive than G3.

Minimum In (M1 P1) is now General Population Level 2 (G2P2)
   If serving fifty years or more, 3G must have served ten years flat, on 3G must have served five years flat.

Minimum Out (M0 P0) is now General Population Level 1 (G1, P1)
   Must be within twenty-four months of parole eligibility or discharge

Medical and Dental Services
Offered TDCJ Inmates

I. Primary Care

This is the inmate's first point of contact with the health care system. This level offers medical care for the large number of conditions that frequently occur in the population and which do not require sophisticated technical capability to diagnose or treat. This level also provides for the triage and referral of patients to the secondary level, which offers more specialized diagnostic procedures and treatment. *All* units in the TDCJ-ID offer at least primary care.

Services provided:

  A. Self-care—personal hygiene and care for a condition that can be self-treated.

  B. First aid services—services for a minor condition that can be treated with over-the-counter products by uncredentialed person trained in first aid.

  C. Basic Ambulatory Clinic Outpatient Services:

    1. Medical services offered:

      a) medication administration

      b) screening physical exams

      c) immunizations

      d) personal health and hygiene counseling

      e) nutrition counseling

      f) basic history and physical exams and evaluation

      g) diagnosis and treatment of simple illnesses and minor injuries

      h) specimen collection and basic laboratory procedures

      i) basic radiology services (chest, abdomen, KUB, extremities)

      j) eyeglass fittings

      k) EKGs

      l) Basic respiratory therapy services

m) Minor surgical procedures (suturing of simple lacerations, simple incision and drainage, uncomplicated removal of foreign bodies)

2. Dental services offered
   a) fillings and scalings
   b) extractions
   c) impactions
   d) alveolectomies
   e) impressions
   f) oral prosthetics

Primary care also includes periodic screening (annual TB screenings, pap smears, etc.,) treatment sessions, basic emergency stabilization and transport, as well as medical observation services which, if ordered by physician, are provided in beds located in the unit medical department.

II. Secondary Care

Secondary level care is the mid-level of care, which provides both outpatient specialty services and/or infirmary inpatient services. Infirmaries are where inpatient services are rendered around-the-clock by nurses for patients needing short-term inpatient care for pre-or post-hospitalization care. *Basic* care means an RN supervisor on the day shift with an LVN charge nurse on the other two shifts. *Skilled* nursing care means an RN on all three shifts.

Two distinct echelons of outpatient care are provided at larger/special population or location units and *cluster units* (lower care) and *regional medical facilities*, which provide higher care.

Cluster units provide limited specialty outpatient services and basic nursing inpatient services to the population assigned to its own unit as well as nearby units. The determination of sites for cluster units is based on such features as geographic location, associated travel times, inmate medical and security characteristics, facility design, and staffing requirements. Cluster units provide the following services in addition to those provided by a basic primary level unit:

A. limited specialty outpatient services

B. herapeutic diet services

C. casting of simple uncomplicated fractures

D. optometry services, including basic vision and refractions

E. specimen collection and limited laboratory services, including complete hematology; complete urines; serum glucose; simple culturing; limited chemistries

F. limited radiology services, including spine series; skull series

G. limited physical medicine services, including hydrotherapy for arms, legs and hips

H. computerized EKG interpretations

Regional Medical Facilities provide moderate consultative specialty outpatient services combined with infirmary services, which have greater bed capacity, skilled nursing services, and moderate medical services. It is assumed that John Sealy Hospital in Galveston will be used as the principal referral site for off-site outpatient specialty consultations. However, in order to ensure due access to specialty consultation, a number of high-volume clinics will be held at the Regional Medical Facilities. Frequency of each clinic will be adjusted according to experienced demand. When providers in a specific specialty are not available, off-site referrals will be made.

The following clinics are among those that may offer services at the Regional Medical Facilities:

A. Internal medicine:

  1. Urology

  2. Dermatology

  3. Otorhinolaringology

  4. Orthopedics

  5. Reconstructive surgery

  6. Opthamology

  7. Oral Surgery

  8. General surgery

  9. Obstetrics and gynecology

B. Moderate surgical services similar to a day surgery "surgicenter," such as:

  1. EMT surgery

  2. Plastic reconstructive surgery

  3. Podiatric surgery

    4. Surgery

    5. Oral surgery

    6. Ophthalmic surgery

C. Moderate laboratory services, such as:

    1. Hematology—CBC, retic count, platelet count, sedimentation rate, prothrobin time and PTT

    2. Serology—VDRL or RPR, RA, monospot, C-reactive protein, LE, febrile afflutination, blood type and Rh

    3. Chemistry—BUN, biliribin, glucose, amylasee, albumin, alkaline phosphatase, calcium, creatinine, globulin, phosphorous, uric acid, total protein, potassium and sodium

    4. Parasitology—Fecal exams for occult blood and stool culture and sensitivity

    5. Bacteriology—Body fluids, KOH fungus culture, CG gram stains and cultures, AFB stains and cultures

D. Moderate radiology services, including fluoroscopy.

E. Moderate physical medicine services—Electrotherapy (ultrasound, electrostimulator, radiant heat and diathermy); Hydrotherapy (whirlpool, paraffin, and oil bath); Physical medicine (bicycle exercise, walker training, quad training and exercise, cervical traction, active and passive range of motion exercise, active rehab, and massage); Exercise (active, passive, flexion and extension parallel bars, shoulder, wheel, overhead wall pulley, treadmill, gait training, stair training and muscle training.)

F. Moderate occupational therapy services—Eating and utensil handling, Barrier symbol reading, and Hygiene training

G. Moderate speech therapy services.

H. Moderate respiratory therapy services—IPPB, Pulmonary function studies, and Arterial blood gases

 I. Treadmill testing and EEG services

 J. Dialysis, where appropriate

K. Complete pharmacy services and distribution

L. Emergency services offered—emergency care unit equivalent to a Trauma III level emergency service.

(Source: TDC Comprehensive Health Care plan, 1984, attachments 134c, 134d, 134e,134f)

APPENDIX C
Law Library Holdings

Following is a partial listing of the books and manuals that all TDCJ law libraries must offer to remain in compliance with court-ordered stipulations concerning access to courts. Many transfer units and smaller units have mini-law libraries, and they offer less, but most attempt to make up the difference via loan programs with other TDCJ law libraries.

1. Federal Reporter 2d.
2. Federal Reporter 3d w/advance sheets
3. Federal Supplement w/advance sheets
4. Supreme Court Reporter w/interim bound volumes and advance sheets
5. United States Supreme Court Digest
6. South Western Reporter 2d, Texas w/advance sheets
7. Texas Subsequent History Table
8. United States Codes Annotated—Title 18: 19 volumes w/pocket parts; Title 28: 13 volumes w/pocket parts; Title 42: 5 volumes w/ pocket parts
9. Vernon's Texas Statutes and Codes Annotated: 108 volumes w/ pocket parts
10. Vernon's Texas Rules Annotated: 9 volumes w/pocket parts
11. Texas Evidence and Courtroom Handbook
12. Wright's Federal Practice and Procedure, Criminal
13. Corpus Juris Secundum, Criminal only
14. Texas Digest, 2nd Edition; 72 book w/pocket parts
15. Texas Annotated Penal Statutes w/Forms, Branch's 3rd Edition
16. Local rules of the U.S. District Court for Texas Districts
17. Legal Research in a Nutshell
18. West's Law Finder
19. Federal and State Postconviction Remedies and Relief
20. Black's Law Dictionary
21. U.S. Constitution
22. Texas Legal Directories
23. Department of Public Safety Handbook – Texas Criminal Laws

24. Texas Board of Pardons and Paroles Rules

25. Parole in Texas

26. TDCJ-ID Inmate Legal Handbook

27. TDCJ-ID Disciplinary Rules and Procedures for Inmates

28. TDCJ-ID Classification Plan

29. TDCJ-ID Comprehensive Health Care Plan

30. TDCJ-ID AD/SEG Plan

31. TDCJ-ID Use of Force plan

32. Compendium of the law on Prisoner's Rights

33. How to use your West's Texas Digest

34. How to use Shepard's Citations

Pamphlets Available:

a) Federal Civil Procedure and Rules

b) Federal Criminal Procedure and Rules

c) Texas Rules of Court, State

d) Texas Rules of Court, Federal

e) Texas Law Finder

Also available—Assorted stipulations, orders, and reports regarding: *Ruiz b. Estelle*; *Lamar v.Coffield*; *Ruiz,et al v. Procunier*; *Ruiz, et al v. Johnson*; and copies of the amended decree. Photocopies of Administrative Memorandums are to be made available to inmates upon request.

(Source: TDCJ-ID Law Library Holdings List)

APPENDIX D
Commissary Spending Limits

As of August 2001, the following limits on commissary spending were in effect for inmates in TDCJ-ID, applied according to custody level.

G1, G2, and G3 Minimum—$75 every two weeks, raised to $100 on certain holidays
G4 Medium—$30 every two weeks
G5 Close—$20 every two weeks
Administrative Segregation:
    Level I—$60 every two weeks
    Level II—one item of each hygiene and correspondence, not to exceed $10, every two weeks
    Level III—correspondence supplies not to exceed $10, every two weeks

(Source; TDCJ-ID Classification plan, Revised Nov. 1999)

APPENDIX E
Recreation Requirements

Following are the minimum hours of recreation to be given each inmate, as agreed to under *Ruiz*. Units may offer more but not less. For these purposes, dayroom time is counted as recreation (rec) time. (In mid-2001, staffing shortages were serving as an excuse for certain units to begin scaling back these requirements.)

G1, G2, and G3 Minimum—Four hours weekday, one of which must be in a gym or outside rec yard. Seven hours weekend, two of which must be in a gym or outside rec yard

G 4 Medium—Four hours weekday, one of which must be in a gym or outside rec yard. Five hours weekend, two of which must be in a gym or outside rec yard

G 5 Close—Two hours daily, outside rec only

Administrative segregation:

    Level I—One hour out-of-cell rec each day, with at least two hours weekly outside; Or two hours out-of-cell rec five days per week, with two hour weekly outside; Or three hours out-of-cell four days per week, with three hours weekly outside. (The Level I schedule will be decided upon by the warden or his/her designee.)

    Level II—One hour of out-of-cell four days per week, with one hour weekly outside

    Level III—One hour of out-of-cell rec three days per week, with one hour weekly outside.

(Source: TDCJ-ID Administrative Segregation Plan, April 2000)

APPENDIX F
Good Conduct Time

Good Conduct time awarded per month is broken down into "regular" and "additional" (allowed for completion of educational and vocational plans) with a total shown.

I. Pre-70th Legislature offenses committed prior to September 1, 1987

Class	Regular	Additional	Total
SAT I	45	0	45
SAT I A	45	5	50
SAT I B	45	10	55
SAT I C	45	15	60
SAT II	45	0	45
SAT II A	45	5	50
SAT II B	45	10	55
SAT II C	45	15	60
SAT III	45	0	45
SAT III A	45	5	50
SAT III B	45	10	55
SATIII C	45	15	60
SAT III Const	45	0	45
SAT III A Const	45	5	50
SAT III B Const	45	10	50
SAT III C Const	45	15	60
SAT IV	40	0	40
SAT IV	40	5	45
SAT IV	40	10	50
SAT IV	40	15	55

SAT IV Const	40	0	40
SAT IV A Const	40	5	45
SAT IV B Const	40	10	50
SAT IV C Const	40	15	55
Line I	20	0	20
Line I A	20	5	25
Line I B	20	10	30
Line I C	20	15	35
Line II	10	0	10
Line III	0	0	0

II. Post-70th Legislature offenses committed on or after September 1, 1987

Class	Regular	Additional	Total
SAT I	30	15	45
SAT II	30	15	45
SAT III	30	15	45
SAT IV	25	15	40
Line I	20	15	35
Line II	10	15	25
Line III	0	0	0

(Source: TDCJ-ID Administrative Directive 04.10, September 1, 1998)

APPENDIX G
Parole Officials

There are two distinct entities that concern themselves with parole in Texas—the Parole Division of the TDCJ and the Board of Pardons and Paroles. The first agency actually oversees inmates who have been released. Ex-cons report to them, and it is their staffers who visit homes and ensure that the provisions of parole (set by the Board) are actually met. The second is an independent agency whose primary role is the discretionary release of inmates from prison, along with revocation of released prisoners.

You may reach the Parole Division at:

TDCJ-ID Parole Division
8610 Shoal Creek Blvd.
P.O. Box 13401, Capitol Station
Austin, TX 78711
(512) 406-5200
FAX (512) 406-5858

The members of the Board of Pardons and Paroles are appointed by the governor to six-year terms, which are staggered so all do not expire at the same time. You may write or call the Board members, or the chairman, at the following addresses:

Texas Board of Pardons and Paroles
209 W. 14th Street, Suite 500
Austin, TX 78701
(mailing address)
P.O. Box 13401
Austin, TX 78711-3401
Telephone (512) 463-1679
FAX (512) 463-8120

Address for the offices of the Board members of the Texas Board of Pardons and Paroles follow:

Abilene Office
100 Chestnut, Suite 105
Abilene, TX 79602
(915) 676-4204

Amarillo Office
5809 S. Western, Suite 140
Amarillo, TX 79110
Telephone (806) 359-7656
FAX (806) 358-6455

Angleton Office
1212 North Velasco, Suite 201
Angleton, TX 77515
Telephone (409) 849-3031
FAX (409) 849-8741

Gatesville Office
3404 S. State Hwy. 36
Gatesville, TX 76528
Telephone (254) 865-8870
FAX (254) 865-2629

Huntsville Office
1300 11th, Suite 505
or P.O. Box 599
Huntsville, TX 77340
Telephone (409) 291-2162
FAX (409) 291-8367

Palestine Office
207 E Reagan
Palestine, TX 75801
Telephone (903)723-1068
FAX (903) 723-1441

San Antonio Office
420 S. Main
San Antonio, TX 78204
Telephone (210) 226-1114

APPENDIX H
Administrative Offices and Unit Profiles

Administrative Offices:

Offender Grievances
901 Normal Park, Suit 101A
Huntsville, TX 77342
(936) 293-4065

Risk Management (Safety)
P.O. Box 99
Huntsville, TX 77342
(936) 437-2500

Pest Control
One Circle Drive
Sugarland, TX 77478
(281) 490-1152

Chaplaincy
2503 Lake Rd., Suite 19
Huntsville, TX 77340
(936) 437-5050

Health Services
3009 Highway 30 West
Huntsville, TX 77340
(936) 437-3570

Inner Change (Religious Program)
P.O. Box 99
Huntsville, TX 77342
(936) 294-2183

Preventive Medicine (HIV/Hepatitis C)
3009 Highway 30 West
Huntsville, TX 77340
(936) 437-3570

Offender Mail System
P.O. Box 99
Huntsville, TX 77342
(936) 294-6908

Institutional Division (Ad/seg, Disc.)
P.O. Box 99
Huntsville, TX 77342
(936) 294-2169

Sex Offender Treatment Program
P.O. Box 38
Huntsville, TX 77344
(936) 295-6331 ext. 241

Laundry & Food Services
P.O. Box 99
Huntsville, TX 77342
(936) 437-5150

Substance Abuse Treatment
1600 Financial Plaza, Suite 370
Huntsville, TX 77340
(936) 437-2850

Classification & Records (good time, status)
P.O. Box 99
Huntsville, TX 77342
(936) 294-6231

Windham School District (GED, college)
P.O. Box 40
Huntsville, TX 77342
(936) 291-5303

Internal Affairs
P.O. Box 99
Huntsville, TX 77342
(936) 294-6716

State Counsel for Offenders (for
immigration, detainers)
P.O. Box 4005
Huntsville, TX 77342
(936) 437-5206

Unit Profiles:

The following information was taken from TDCJ's website (http://
www.tdcj.state.tx.us) and was up to date as of June 2000. It has been
divided into sections, by type of facility. First are the fifty-three prison
units run by TDCJ; following, by type of facility, are the six TDCJ Medi-
cal/Psychiatric units; the fourteen TDCJ Transfer Facilities; the twelve
State Jails; the nine Substance Abuse Felony Punishment Facilities; and
the nineteen private prisons. For each facility, I have provided the following information:

A. Unit name, address and phone number. It would be futile to give
   unit officials' names (wardens, majors, etc.) because they change
   so frequently. A call to a unit and request to speak with a particular official will be rewarded if you are persistent.
B. OP—Offender Population
C. IND—Industry. The more industries located on a given unit, the
   more semi-skilled and highly skilled jobs available to inmates.
D. CTE—Career and Technology. Unless indicated otherwise, a
   facility offers the basic Windham programs (literacy/GED, Pre-
   release, Special Ed., Project RIO). I will not list them. I will list
   the Career and Technology (CTE) programs, which are
   Windham's vocational courses. As of June 2000, Windham
   offered thirty-seven CTE courses, I have numbered them as
   follows:
   1. Auto Collision Repair & Refinishing Technology
   2. Auto Specialization/Air Conditioning & Heating
   3. Auto Specialization/Brakes
   4. Auto Specialization/Electronics
   5. Auto Specialization/Engine Performance
   6. Auto Specialization/Radiator Repair

7. Auto Specialization/Transmission Repair

8. Barbering

9. Bricklaying

10. Business Computer Information Systems

11. Business Support Systems

12. Computer Applications

13. Computer Maintenance Technician

14. Construction Carpentry

15. Culinary Arts

16. Custodial Technician

17. Diesel Mechanics

18. Diversified Career Preparation

19. Electrical Trades

20. Floral Design & Interior Design Management

21. Graphic Arts

22. Heating/Ventilation/Air Conditioning & Refrigeration

23. Horticulture

24. Institutional Maintenance and Management Services

25. Landscape Design/Construction/Maintenance

26. Machine Shop

27. Major Appliance Service Technicians

28. Mill & Cabinetmaking

29. Personal & Family Development

30. Paint & Decorating

31. Piping Trades/Plumbing

32. Plant Maintenance

33. Sheet Metal

34. Small Engine Repair

35. Technological Intro to Computer Aided Drafting

36. Truck Driving

37. Welding

E. CA—College Academics. Lists the name of a college/university that offers college courses at that unit.

F. CV—College Vocational. Lists the vocational courses offered by the college on that unit. The college vocational courses offered on TDCJ units are numbered as follows:

1. Air Conditioning & Refrigeration
2. Auto Body
3. Auto Electronic
4. Auto Mechanics
5. Auto Transmission
6. Building Maintenance Technician
7. Computer Repair
8. Culinary Arts
9. Data Processing
10. Diesel Mechanics
11. Drafting
12. Electronics
13. Graphic Arts
14. Horticulture
15. Masonry
16. Office Administration
17. Truck Driving
18. Upholstery
19. Welding

Unit Profiles:

Allred
2101 FM369 North
Iowa Park, TX 76367
(940) 855-7477
OP—3,658 males
IND—none
CTE—5, 9, 14, 31, 34
CA—none
CV – none

Baten
1995 Hilton Road
Pampa, TX 79065
(806) 665-7070
OP—398 males
IND, CTE, CA, and CV—none

Beto
P.O. Box 128
Tennessee Colony, TX 75880
OP—3,357 males
(903) 928-2217
IND—Metal sign shop
CTE—9, 11, 14, 28, 31, 37
CA—Trinity Valley Community (2-yr)
CV—7, 9, 11, 12

Boyd
Route 2, Box 500
Teague, TX 75860
(254) 739-5555
OP—1,287 males
IND—Stainless Steel Plant
CTE—7, 14, 23, 24, 30
CA and CV—none

Briscoe
1459 West Hwy. 85
Dilley, TX 78017
(830) 965-4444
OP—1,334 males
IND—Furniture Factory
CTE—14, 19, 25
CA and CV—none

Byrd (Diagnostic)
P.O. Box 100
Huntsville, TX 77342
(936) 295-5768
OP—908 Males
IND—Boyd Ind. Warehouse
CTE, CA, and CV—none

Central
One Circle Drive
Sugarland, TX 77478
(281) 491-2146
OP—1,012 males
IND—Soap & Detergent Factory
CTE—18, 23, 36
CA—Alvin Community College (2-yr)
CV—14

Clemens
11034 Hwy. 36
Brazoria, TX 77422
(979) 798-2188
OP—1,181 males
IND—none
CTE—6, 8, 10, 31
CA and CV—none

Clements
9601 Spur 591
Amarillo, TX 79107-9606
(806) 381-7080
OP—3,056 males
IND—Shoe Factory
CTE—10, 14, 16, 18, 19, 23, 28, 35
CA—none
CV—4, 9, 11

Coffield
Route 1, Box 150
Tennessee Colony, TX 75884
(903) 928-2211
OP—4,115
IND—Metal Fabrication Shop
CTE—3, 5, 10, 14
CA—Trinity Valley Community (2-yr)

Connally
HC 67, Box 115
Kenedy, TX 78119
(830) 583-4003
OP—2,834 males
IND—none
CTE—13, 14, 17, 19, 31, 34
CA and CV—none

Dalhart
HCR 4, Box 4000
Dalhart, TX 79022
(806) 249-8655
OP—1,342 males
IND—none
CTE—14, 19, 31
CA and CV—none

Daniel
938 South FM 1673
Snyder, TX 79549
(915) 573-1114
OP—1,318 males
IND—Modular Furniture Factory
CTE—3, 14, 16
CA—Western Texas College (2 yr.)
CV—4, 14

Darrington
59 Darrington Road
Rosharon, TX 77583
(281) 595-3465
OP—1,838 males
IND—Tire Recapping Plant
CTE—10, 22
CA—Alvin Community College (2 yr.)
CV—4, 9, 19

Eastham
P.O. Box 16
Lovelady, TX 75851
(936) 636-7321
OP—2,240 males
IND—Garment Factory
CTE—5, 30, 34
CA and CV—none

Ellis (Ellis I Unit)
Huntsville, TX 77343
(936) 295-5756
OP—2,390 males
IND—Bus Repair Shop, Garment Factory,
Woodworking Shop
CTE—13
CA—Lee College (2 yr.), Sam Houston
State (4 yr.)
CV—2, 10, 12, 14, 18

Estelle
264 FM 3478
Huntsville, TX 77320
(936) 291-4200
OP—2,973 males
IND—Textile Mill
CTE—9, 10, 17, 18, 23, 30, 35
CA—Lee College (2 yr.)
CV—9

Ferguson
12120 Savage Drive
Midway, TX 75852
(409) 348-3751
OP—2,392 males
IND—Mapping Facility, Mop & Broom
Factory
CTE—10, 14, 15, 19, 26, 28, 31, 35, 37
CA—Lee College (2 yr.)
CV—none

Gatesville
1401 State School Rd.
Gatesville, TX 76599-2999
(254) 865-8431
OP—2, 051 females
IND—none
CTE—14, 24, 29, 37
CA—Central Texas College (2 yr.),
Tarleton State University (4 yr.)
CV—13, 16

Goree
7504 Hwy. 75 South
Huntsville, TX 77344
(936) 295-6331
OP—1,087 males (w/transient females)
IND—none
CTE, CA, and CV—none
(Goree serves as the psychological evalu-
ation Unit, as the adjunct to Byrd)

Hightower
Route 3, Box 9800
Dayton, TX 77535
(936) 258-8013
OP—1,329 males
IND—Garment Factory
CTE—14, 27
CA—Lee College (2 yr.)
CV—1, 14

Hilltop
1500 State School Rd
Gatesville, TX 76598-2996
(254) 865-8901
OP—625 females
IND—Garment Factory
CTE—21
CA—none
CV—9

Hobby
Route 2, Box 600
Marlin, TX 76661
(254) 883-5561
OP—1,325 females
IND—Print Shop
CTE—2, 3, 27, 31
CA and CV—none

Hughes
Route 2, Box 4400
Gatesville, TX 76597
(254) 865-6663
OP—3,865 males
IND – Garment Factory
CTE—3, 5, 16, 22, 31
CA—Central Texas (2 yr.), Tarleton State
University (4 yr.)
CV—1, 8

Huntsville (Walls)
P.0. Box 32
Huntsville, TX 77348
(936) 437-1975
OP—1,553 males
IND—Textile Mill, Garment Factories
Warehouse, Media Center
CTE—10
CA—Lee College (2 yr.), Sam Houston
State (4 yr.)
CV—4, 9

Jester III Unit
Richmond, TX 77469
(281) 277-7000
OP—1,085 males
IND—Garment Factory
CTE—10, 37
CA—Alvin Community College (2 yr.)
CV—4, 9
(This unit has 128 barrier-free beds and
accepts inmates with mobility problems)

Jordan
1992 Hilton Rd.
Pampa, TX 79065
(806) 665-7070
OP—999 males
IND—Sewing Factory
CTE—19, 27, 32
CA—Clarendon College (2 yr.)
CV—none

Leblanc
3695 FM 3514
Beaumont, TX 77705
(409) 724-1515
OP—950 males
IND—none
CTE and CV—none
CA—Lamar State College (2 yr.)
(This unit is designated as a pre-release
substance abuse program unit.)

Lewis
P.O. Box 9000
Woodville, TX 75990
(409) 283-8181
OP—2,157 males
IND—Woodworking Shop
CTE—19, 22, 28
CA and CV—none

Luther
1800 Luther Drive
Navasota, TX 77869
(936) 825-7547
OP—1,296 males
IND—Stainless Steel Plant
CTE—3, 5, 19, 23, 37
CA—Blinn College (2 yr.)
CV—none

Lynaugh
900 GM 2937
Fort Stockton, TX 79735
OP—1,356 males
IND – none
CTE—2, 19, 31
CA and CV—none

McConnell
3001 South Emily Dr.
Beeville, TX 78102
(361) 362-2300
OP—2,785 males
ND – Garment Factory
CTE—4, 10, 16, 22
CA—Coastal Bend College (2 yr.)
CV—1, 9, 14, 15

Michael
P.O. Box 4500
Tennessee Colony, TX 75866
(903) 928-2311
OP—3,193 males
IND—Metal Fabrication Plant
CTE—4, 11, 31, 33
CA—Trinity Valley Comm. College (2 yr.)
CV—1, 9, 14, 15

Mountain View
2305 Ransom Rd.
Gatesville, TX 76528
(254) 865 7226
OP—605 females
IND—Bindery & Braille Facility
CTE—10, 11, 13, 20, 23
CA—Central Texas College (2 yr.), Tarleton State U. (4 yr.)

Murray
1916 North Hwy. 36 Bypass
Gatesville, TX 76596
(254) 865-2000
OP—1,302 females
IND, CA, and CV—none
CTE—16

Neal
9055 Spur 591
Amarillo, TX 79107-9696
(806) 383-1175
OP—1,347 males
IND—none
CTE—10, 14, 16
CA—none
CV—9

Pack
2400 Wallace Pack Rd.
Navasota, TX 77868
(936) 825-3728
OP—1,495 males
IND—none
CTE—10, 14, 21, 22
CA—Blinn College
CV—none

Polunsky
12002 FM 350 South
Livingston, TX 77351
(936) 967-8082
OP—2,888 males
IND—Furniture Factory
CTE—7, 22, 28, 32
CA and CV—none

Powledge
Route 2, Box 2250
Palestine, TX 75882
(903) 723-5074
OP—1,119 males
IND—Metal Fabrication Plant
CTE—1, 14, 18, 30, 37
CA—Trinity Valley Community College
(2 yr.)
CV—2, 19

Ramsey I
1100 FM 655
Rosharon,TX 77583
(281) 595-3491
OP—1,750 males
IND—Furniture Refinishing Factory
CTE—2, 3, 18, 28
CA—Alvin Community College (2 yr.),
University of Houston-Clear Lake (4 yr.
and graduate—MA)

Ramsey II
1200 FM 655
Rosharon, TX 77583
(281) 595-3413
OP—1,150
IND—none
CTE—13, 14, 34, 35
CA—Alvin Community College (2 yr.)
CV—7

Retrieve
Route 5, Box 1500
Angleton, TX 77515
(979) 849-9306
OP—1,068 males
IND—none
CTE—25
CA and CV—none

Roach
Route 2, Box 500
Childress, TX 79201
(940) 937-6364
OP—1,459 males
IND—Soap Factory
CTE—14, 19, 22, 25
CA—Clarendon College (2 yr.)
CV—none

Robertson
12071 FM 3522
Abilene, TX 79601
(915) 548-9035
OP—2,877 males
IND—Garment Factory
CTE—5, 13, 16, 22, 32, 34
CA and CV—none

Smith
1313 CR 19
Lamesa, TX 79331
(806) 872-6741
OP—2,095
IND—Mattress Factory
CTE—14, 19, 27, 31
CV—none

Stevenson
1525 FM 766
Cuero, TX 77954
(361) 275-2075
OP—1,328 males
IND—Furniture Factory
CTE—14, 18, 19, 31, 32
CA—Coastal Bend College (2 yr.)
CV—none

Stiles
3060 FM 3514
Beaumont, TX 77705
(409) 722-5255
OP – 2,856 males
IND—Precision Sheet Metal Plant
CTE—4, 10, 14, 26, 27
CA—Lamar University-Port Arthur (2 yr.)
CV—3, 5, 9

Telford
P.O. Box 9200
New Boston, TX 75570
(903) 628-3171
OP—2,803 males
IND—none
CTE—10, 13, 32, 34
CA and CV—none

Terrell
1300 FM 655
Rosharon, TX 77583
(281) 595-3481
OP—1,579 males
IND—none
CTE—16, 18, 19, 37
CA—Alvin Community College (2 yr.)
CV—9

Torres
125 Private Rd. 4303
Hondo, TX 78861
(830) 426-5325
OP—1,323 males
IND—Print Shop
CTE—16, 18, 22, 34
CA—Southwest Texas Junior College (2 yr.)
CV—none

Vance
Carol Vance Unit
Route 2
(281) 277-3030
OP—325 males
IND, CTE, CA, and CV—none
(This unit houses the InnerChange Faith-Based Treatment Program)

Wallace
P.O. Box 2000
Colorado City, TX 79512
(915) 728-2162
OP—1,686 males
IND—Garment Factory
CTE—3, 5, 14, 18
CA—Western Texas College (2 yr.)
CV—1, 14

Wynne Unit
Huntsville, TX 77349
(936) 295-9126
OP—2,607 males
IND—Box Factory, Computer Recovery
Facility, License Plate Plant, Mattress
Factory, Signage/Plastics Facility,
Validation Sticker Plant
CTE—13, 17, 18, 34, 35, 37
CA—Lee College (2 yr.)
CV—12, 17, 19

Medical/ Psychiatric Units

None of these facilities have college academics, college vocational or industry.

Galveston
P.O. Box 48
Substation #1
(409)772-2875
OP—17 females and 132 males
CTE—none
(This unit is designated as a Medical Facility.)

Montford
8602 Peach Street
Lubbock, TX 79404
(806) 745-1021
OP—965 males
CTE—11
(This unit is designated as a Psychiatric Facility)

Hodge
P.O. Box 999
Rusk, TX 75785
(903) 683-5781
OP—876 males
CTE—16, 23, 25, 29
(This unit houses TDCJ's Mentally
Retarded Offender Program)

Skyview
P.O. Box 999
Rusk, TX 75785
(903) 683-5781
OP—61 females and 427 males
CTE—none
(This unit is designated as a Psychiatric Facility)

Texas City
Route 4 Box 1174
Dickenson, TX 77539
(409) 948-0024
OP—41 females and 336 males
CTE—none
(This unit is designated as a Medical
Facility. It is where pregnant inmates are
assigned until they give birth.)

Jester IV
Richmond, TX 77469-8549
(281) 277-3700
OP—510 males
CTE—none
(This unit is designated as a Psychiatric Facility)

Transfer Units

None of these units have industry or college vocational. An inmate's maximum stay here will be two years prior to being assigned to a regular prison unit. These units are mostly exempt from *Ruiz v Estelle* stipulations.

Cotulla
HC 62 Box 100
Cotulla, TX 78014
(830) 879-3077
OP—560 males
CTE and CA—none

Duncan
1502 South First St.
Diboll, TX 75941
(936) 829-2616
OP—537 males
CTE—14
CA—none

Fort Stockton
1500 IH-10 East
Fort Stockton, TX 79735
(915) 336-7676
OP—539 males
CTE and CA—none

Garza East
HC 02 Box 985
Beeville, TX 78102
(361) 358-9890
OP—2,021 males
CTE and CA—none

Garza West
HC 02 Box 995
Beeville, TX 78102
(361) 358-9890
OP—2,020 males
CTE and C A—none

Goodman
Route 1 Box 273
Jasper, TX 75951
(409) 383-0012
OP—599 males
CTE—0
CA—none

Gurney
P.O. Box 6400
Tennessee Colony, TX 75861
(903) 928-3118
OP—1,864 males
CTE—16, 31

Holliday
295 IH-45 North
Huntsville, TX 77320-8200
(936) 295-8200
OP—1,847 males
CTE—25
CA—none

Middleton
13055 FM 3522
Abilene, TX 79601
(915) 548-9075
OP—1,880 males
CTE—16
CA—none

Moore, Choice
1700 North FM 87
Bonham, TX 75418
(903) 583-4464
OP—1,190 males
CTE and CA—none

Rudd
2004 Lamesa Highway
Brownfield, TX 79316
(806) 637-4470
OP—586 males
CTE and CA—none

Tulia
HCR 3 Box 5C
Tulia, TX 79008
(806) 995-4109
OP—558 males
CTE and CA—none

Segovia
1201 El Cibolo Rd.
Edinburg, TX   78539
(956) 316-2400
OP—1,947 males
CTE—10, 11, 16
CA—none

Ware
P.O. Box 2500
Colorado City, TX 79512
(915) 728-2162
OP—872 males
CTE—14, 25
CA—Western Texas College

State Jails

None of these facilities have Industry or college vocational. These units are supposedly reserved for inmates who have committed felonies that carry sentences explicitly stating assignment to a state jail, with lengths of no more than a few years.

Cole
3801 Silo Road
Bonham, TX 75418
telephone?
OP—861 males
CTE—12, 19, 26
CA—none

Formby
970 County Road AA
Plainview, TX 79027
(806) 296-2448
OP—1,044 males
CTE—14, 16
CA—none

Dominguez
6535 Cagnon Road
San Antonio, TX 78252-2202
(210) 675-6620
OP—2,061 males
CTE—13, 35
CA—Palo Alto College (2 yr.)

Gist
3295 FM 3514
Beaumont, TX 77705
(409) 727-8400
OP—2,063 males
CTE—10, 16
CA—none

Hutchins
1500 East Langdon Road
Dallas, TX 75241
(972) 225-1304
OP—2,019 males
CTE—10, 35
CA—none

Kegans
707 Top Street
Houston, TX 77002
(713) 224-6584
OP—659 males
CTE and CA—none

Lopez
1203 El Cibolo Rd.
Edinburg, TX 78539-9334
(956) 316-3810
OP—1,059 males
CTE—14, 19
CA—none

Lychner
2350 Atascocita Rd.
Humble, TX 77396
(281)454-5036
OP—2,058 males
CTE—10, 16, 35
CA—none

Plane
Route 3 Box 8000B
Dayton, TX 77535
OP—2,094
CTE—10, 23
CA—none

Sanchez
3901 State Jail Road
El Paso, TX 79938-8456
(915) 856-0046
OP—1,028 males
CTE—22, 31

Travis County
8101 FM 969
Austin, TX 78724
(512) 926-4482
OP—959 males
CTE—10
CA—none

Woodman
1210 Coryell City Road
Gatesville, TX 76528
(254) 865-9398
OP—821 females
CTE—16, 30
CA—none

Substance Abuse Felony Punishment Facilities

None of these units have industry, college academic or college vocational. Assignment to these units is dictated by parole board as a condition of release. Inmates receiving discipinary cases may be returned to regular units.

Glossbrenner
623 South FM 1329
San Diego, TX 78384
(361) 279-2705
OP—500 males
CTE—none

Halbert
P.O. Box 923
Burnet, TX 78611
(512) 756-6171
OP—447 females
CTE—none

Havins
P.O. Box 90401
Brownwood, TX 76804-4401
(915) 643-5575
OP—515 males
CTE—none

Henley
Route 3 Box 7000B
Dayton, TX 77535
(936) 258-2476
OP—467 females
CTE—10

Jester I
Richmond, TX 77469
(281) 277-3030
OP—316 males
CTE—none

Johnston
703 Airport Road
Winnsboro, TX 75494
(903) 342-6166
OP—498 males
CTE—2, 25

Ney
114 Private Road 4304
Hondo, TX 78861-3812
(830) 426-8030
OP—492 males
CTE—none

Sayle
4176 FM 1800
Breckenridge, TX 76424-7301
(254) 559-1581
OP—519 males
CTE—none

Wheeler
4300 East Fifth Street
Plainview, TX 79072
(806) 293-1081
OP—486 males
CTE—none

Private Prisons

None of these units, other than Lockhart, have industry. These units offer two types of vocational courses (VOC), both of which I have listed in their entirety. These units are run by private corporations, for profit. They are not administered by TDCJ.

Cleveland
P.O. Box 1678
Cleveland, TX 77328
(281) 592-9559
OP—520 males
VOC—AC & Refrigeration, Horticulture
CA—Lee College
CV—Computer Science, Desk Top
Publishing

Diboll
1604 South First Street
Diboll, TX 75941
(936) 829-2295
OP—517 males
VOC—AC & Refrigeration, Business,
Carpentry, Horticulture
CA—Angelina College (2 yr.)
CV—AC & Refrigeration, College
Speech

Estes
1100 Hwy. 1807
Venus, TX 76084
(972) 366-3334
OP—1,000 males
VOC—Building trades, Business
Computer Applications, Business
Computer , Programming, Electrical
Trades, Food Service , Horticulture,
Interior Finishing, Plumbing

Kyle
701 IH-35 South
Kyle, TX 78640
(512) 268-0079
OP—501 males
CA—Southwest Texas State University
(4 yr.)
CV—Basic Office Technology
(This unit is designated as a Substance
Abuse Treatment facility)

Moore, B.
8500 North FM 3053
Overton, TX 75864
(903) 834-6186
OP—496 males
VC—Basic Computer, Computer
Keyboarding, Culinary Arts, Custodial
Maintenance, Electrical Trades
CA—Kilgore College (2 yr.)
CV—Electrical Industrial Maintenance

Privately Operated State Jails

Bartlett
P.O. Box 650
Bartlett, TX 76511
(254) 527-3300
OP—966 males
VOC—Building Maintenance, Carpentry,
Computer Applications, Commercial
Wiring, Culinary Arts, Drafting,
Horticulture, Industrial Cleaning,
Industrial Electronics, Industrial
Maintenance
CA and CV—none

Bradshaw
P.O. Box 9000
Henderson, TX 75653-9000
(903) 655-0880
OP—1,684 males
VOC—Building Maintenance,
Cabinetmaking, Carpentry, Culinary
Arts, Electrical Wiring, Horticulture
CA—none
CV—Building Maintenance, Computer
Literacy, Masonry, Woodworking,
Master Gardner-Horticulture

Dawson
P.O. Box 605675
Dallas, TX 75265
(214) 744-4422
OP—716 females and 1,212 males
VOC—Computer Applications, Culinary
Arts, Employability Skills Course,
Industrial Electronics, Industrial
Maintenance
CA and CV—none

Lindsey
1137 Old Post Oak Road
Jacksboro, TX 76458
(940) 567-2272
OP—1,008 males
VOC—Building Maintenance, Computer
Applications, Horticulture, Industrial
Cleaning
CA and CV—none

Willacy County
1695 South Buffalo Drive
Raymondville, TX 78580
(956) 689-4900
OP—1,007 males
VOC—Computer Applications, Horticulture, Small Engine Repair

Privately Operated Pre-Parole Transfer Facilities

Bridgeport
222 Lake Road
Bridgeport, TX 76426
(940) 683-2162
OP—186 female
VOC—Accounting, Industrial Cleaning/
Maintenance
CA and CV—none

Mineral Wells
759 Heintzelman Road
Mineral Wells, TX 76067
(940) 325-6933
OP—2,060 males
VOC—Basic Office Technology,
Computer Systems Technology, Construc-
tion, Culinary Arts, Landscaping

Privately Operated Intermediate Sanction Facilities

Central Texas
218 South Laredo Street
San Antonio, TX 78207
(210) 227-5600
OP—108 females and 36 males
CA, CV and VOC—none

South Texas
1511 Preston Road
Houston, TX 77002
(713) 223-0601
OP—429 males
CA, CV and VOC—none

North Texas
4700 Blue Mound Road
Fort Worth, TX 76106
(817) 740-0180
OP—373 males
CA, CV and VOC—none

West Texas
2002 Lamesa Highway
Brownfield, TX 79316
(806) 637-4032
OP—176 males
VOC—Food Service
CA and CV—none

Privately Operated Multi-Use Facilities

El Paso
1700 Horizon Blvd.
El Paso, TX 79927
(915) 852-1505
OP—222 males
CA, CV, and VOC—none

La Villa
1300 Hwy. 107
La Villa, TX 78562
(956) 262-4142
CA, CV, and VOC—none

Privately Operated Work Program

Lockhart
P.O. Box 1170
Lockhart, TX 78644
(512) 398-3480
OP—495 females and 495 males
VOC—Basic Office Technology,
Computer Systems Technology, Desk
Top Publishing, Horticulture, PIE
Industry Training
CA and CV—none
IND—Manufacture of Electronic Circuit
Boards and Air Conditioner Parts,
certified under the Private Sector/Prison
Industries Enhancement Program
(This is the only Texas prison unit to pay
inmates for their labor in this industry)

APPENDIX I
Resource List

Following is a list of some organizations that offer services and assistance to prisoners and their families. Many of them offer other resource lists, generally in an area related to what services they extend. By asking them for resource lists, you can build a network of organizations suited to your particular needs.

Texas Inmate Families Association (TIFA)
P.O. Box 181253
Austin, TX 78718-1253
(512) 695-3031
www.tifa.org
Advocacy group that provides support and resources for families of Texas prisoners. This organization works directly with prisoners' family members, not prisoners. Has chapters throughout Texas and lobbies for change in the legislature, and often meets with top prison officials.

Info, Inc.
Inmate Families Organization, Inc.
P.O. Box 788
Manchaca, TX 78652
www.flash.net/infoinc
Advocacy group similar to TIFA, although newer.

Texas Citizens United for Rehabilitation of Errants (CURE)
P.O. Box 12623
Austin, TX 78711
Offshoot of national organization dedicated to organizing prisoners, their families and others for education and advocacy in criminal justice issues. Publishes quarterly newsletter, free to inmates.

Texas Association of X-offenders (TAX)
P.O. Box 1168
Crockett, TX 75835
Faith-based criminal recovery and relapse prevention program that targets adult offenders, parolees, probationers, and ex-offenders. There are several TAX chapters throughout the state.

The Prison Show
KPFT-90.1 FM
419 Lovett Blvd.
Houston, TX 77006
Friday night staple for South Texas prisoners, is heard from 9 P.M. to 11 P.M. on the Houston Pacifica radio station KPFT. Ray Hill, the program's host, is a former convict turned advocate for unpopular causes, including the plight of Texas inmates.

The ACLU National Prison Project
1875 Connecticut Ave., NW, Suite 410
Washington, DC 20009
The American Civil Liberties Union National Prison Project publishes *The Journal*, a quarterly publication with in-depth analysis of significant new legislation and litigation affecting prisons, reports on AIDS and HIV in prison, and other pertinent information. An annual subscription costs two dollars for inmates and thirty dollars for free-world subscribers. Write and ask for a complete listing of other publications of interest.

Donna Brorby
The Law Office of Donna Brorby
660 Market street, Suite 300
San Francisco, CA 94104
This law office currently represents the cases of all Texas state inmates in the class action lawsuit, *Ruiz v. Johnson,* et. Al., No. H-78-987, in the United States District Court for the Southern District of Texas.

Vinson & Elkins
Attn: John P. DeGeeter
2300 First City Tower 1001 Fannin St.
Houston, TX 77002-6760
This law office currently represents the cases of all Texas state inmates with the state's motion to terminate the judgment in the class action lawsuit *Guadalupe Guajardo, et.al* v. *James A. Collins, Director, TDCJ-ID, et. al.,* No. H-71-570, in the United States District Court for the Southern District of Texas. (This is the action governing mail and correspondence.)

The Innocence Project
Benjamin N. Cardozo School of Law
Yeshiva University—Brookdale Center
55 Fifth Avenue
New York, NY 10013-4391
This group, which includes criminal defense attorney Barry Scheck, helps wrongly convicted prisoners challenge their convictions.

Centurion Ministries, Inc.
32 Nassau Street, 3rd Floor
Princeton, NJ 08542
This group uses DNA testing to try to help prove the innocence of inmates given the death penalty or life imprisonment.

The Fortune Society
53 West 23rd Street
New York, NY 10010
The Fortune Society produces the Fortune News, a monthly publication dedicated to educating the public about prisons, criminal justice issues, and the root causes of crime. The Fortune News is distributed to inmate subscribers in many of the nation's prison systems.

PEN Prison Writing Program
PEN American Center
568 Broadway
New York, NY 10012
Offers assistance, resource list, correspondence courses, Pen Pal listings, and a yearly writing contest for incarcerated writers. Also provides hundreds of addresses of small presses and publications that solicit fiction, poetry, and articles from beginning writers. An invaluable resource for imprisoned writers.

The Prison Library Project
PMB 128
915-C W. Foothill Blvd.
Claremont, CA 91171-3356
This Prison Library Project (PLP) provides a *Ways and Means* resource list to inmates, upon their request. This list gives addresses to write for various types of help (legal assistance, pen pals, reading materials, GED sources, etc.) The primary mission of PLP is to provide reading material free of charge to inmates, prison chaplains,

libraries, and study groups, as well as to veterans, drug/alcohol recovery groups, to support groups for AIDS patients, and victims of abuse within the immediate community. The PLP sends over 30,000 books and audio cassette tapes to inmates each year.

Women's Prison Book Project
c/o Arise Bookstore
2441 Lyndale Avenue South
Minneapolis, MN 55404
The Women's Prison Book Project sends free reading materials and resources to women in prison. It provides books on a variety of topics including fiction, mysteries, health, self-esteem, recovery, crafts, and parenting. It also provides a resource list for women in prison. To receive books, write the project a letter with the types of books you would like and state any restrictions the prison has on receiving packages.

Studies in the Bible
Webb Chapel Church of Christ
13425 Webb Chapel Rd.
Dallas, TX 75234
Offers free Bible study courses to prisoners. Courses are progressively more in-depth and difficult. Offers certificates of completion to anyone who completes a course, of which there are five. Upon completing all ninety lessons, the student is awarded a gift Bible. Also upon completing the last course, a letter requesting personal contact with a student is sent to a congregation near the student.

Heritage Assembly of God
P.O. Box 150098
Fort Worth, TX 76108
Prison Ministry that offers Bible study courses to any inmate who requests them. Series involves approximately seventy-five lessons, in English and Spanish.

Aleph Institute
9540 Collins Ave.
Surfside, FL 33154
Offers religious instruction to inmates; religious articles; correspondence courses; counseling; and prison advocacy. Is in contact with 2,000 primarily Jewish inmates and provides personal visits to inmate; family support groups; and maintains a network of local contacts in all states.

The Islamic Center
2551 Massachusetts Avenue, N.W.
Washington, DC 20008
Consists of a Masjid, a Reference Only Library, and a bookstore. Provides members of the incarcerated community materials such as; the Holy Quran in Arabic, in Arabic-English, Arabic-Spanish, and all English texts. Provides the reading materials (books on Hadith, How to perform Salaah, etc.) as well as video and audio cassettes and How To guides. Also provides Imams as well as speakers to institutions that request help in providing someone to lead them in al'Jumuah prayers.

The International Sivananda Yogi Vedanta Center
P.O. Box 195
Woodbourne, NY 12788-0195
Sponsors Prison Outreach Project that sends Yoga books and other materials to prisoners who request them. Main book is "The Complete Illustrated Book of Yoga." Once communication is initiated, guidance and help are provided by letter.

National Health Prison Project
32 Greenwood Ave. #$
Quincy, MA 02170-2620
The Natural Health Prison Project provides knowledge to help inmates create a healthful and peaceful body/mind. Provides information on diet, longevity, exercise and self-transformation. Will answer personal questions.

Families Against Mandatory Minimums Foundation
1612 K Street NW
Suite 1400
Washington, DC 20006
Seeks to foster awareness about and fight the spread of Mandatory Minimum sentencing in federal and state prisons.

Write the following organizations for more information about the services they provide, all of which are related to prisons and /or crime:

National Center on Institutions and
Alternatives
3125 Mt. Vernon Avenue
Alexandria, VA 22305

Prison Activist Resource Center
P.O. Box 339
Berkeley, CA 94701
parc@prisonactivist.org

American Friends Service Committee
1501 Cherry Street
Philadelphia, PA 19102
afscinfo@afsc.org

Family and Corrections Network
32 Oak Grove Road
Palmyra, VA 22963
fcn@fnetwork.org
Human Rights Watch
350 Fifth Avenue, 34th Floor
New York, NY 10118-3299
www.hrwyc.org

Real Justice
P.O. Box 229
Bethlehem, PA 18016
usa@realjustice.org

The Sentencing Project
514 10th Street, NW
Suite 100
Washington, DC 20004
staff@sentencingproject.org

The Campaign to Abolish Control Unit Prisons is a coalition of individuals and groups who want to eliminate high security, maximum security, and ad/seg type prison units. For information on the Political Action Committee write:

Lorenzo Kom'boa Ervin, Coordinator
c/o The Rest of the News
2014 Citico Ave.
Chattanooga, TN 37404

Dema Mantooth:East
Nightcrawlers ABC
P.O. Box 1034
Mott Street station
Bronx, NY 10454

Christie Donner: Midwest
Rocky Mountain Peace Ctr.
1523 6th St.
Boulder, CO 80302

Corey Weinstein: West
Pelican Bay Info. Project
2489 Mission St. #28
San Francisco, CA 94110

The following halfway houses are currently under contract with the TDCJ
Parole Division. If for some reason, your inmate family member or friend
can not or should not stay with his family upon parole, you should contact one or more of these halfway houses and try to obtain housing.

Austin Salvation Army
Contact: Robert Taylor
501 East 8th St.
Austin, TX 78767
(512)4762628

El Paso/SCS, Inc.
Contact: Tim West
1650 Horizon Blvd. North
El Paso, TX 79927
(817)535-0853

Beaumont/TMG, Inc.
Contact: Ted Blanchard
2495 Gulf Street
Beaumont, TX 77703
(409)832-6495

Houston/Reid CCF
Contact: Craig Ross
10950 Beaumont Hwy.
Houston, TX 77072
(713)675-4426

Dallas Wayback House
Contact: Al Richard
899 N. Stemmons Fwy.
Dallas, TX 75207
(214)742-1971

La Villa/Albert Sneed MUF
Contact: Jim G. Gant
1300 North Hwy. 107
La Villa, TX 78562
(956)262-4142

Del Valle—Austin/TMG,Inc
Contact: K. Gaddie
3320 South FM 973
Del Valle, TX 78617
(512)386-5174

San Antonio/Salvation Army
Contact: Dr. Klon Kitchen
226 Nolan Street
San Antonio, TX 78202
(210)226-2291

El Paso/Alivian, Inc.
Contact: Chilo Madrid
1069 Socorro Road
El Paso, TX 79927
(817)335-6053

Glossary

3g. On September 1, 1987, the 70th Legislature created the so-called 3g offenses, which at the time were Capital Murder, Aggravated Kidnapping, Aggravated Sexual Assault, Aggravated Robbery, and any offense with an affirmative finding of a weapon.

administrative segregation. Ad/seg is a single-celled, high-security status resulting from— repeated, violent attacks on inmates or staff, especially staff; confirmation as a member of a disruptive group, or gang; a need for protection from other inmates; or attempted escape. An inmate in ad/seg is said to be segged, and is denied all face-to-face interaction with inmates and staff until recommendation from unit officials and approval of the State Classification Committee.

building tender. Inmate guards, who were used by prison officials to perform certain supervisory duties. The building tender system was dismantled as a result of *Ruiz v. Estelle*.

case. A disciplinary write-up, the result of being accused of violating a unit or system-wide rule. Also the charge that resulted in one's sentence. If one is fighting one's case, that means the case is on appeal.

chain. Any incoming or outgoing transfer of prisoners involving state vehicles.

cholo. A mixture of English and Spanish slang.

class. A category that designates how much good time an inmate receives. There are seven classes, these being (from lowest good time earning class to highest) Line Class III, Line Class II, Line Class I, State Approved Trusty (SAT) IV, SAT III, SAT II, and SAT I.

concurrent vs. consecutive. Inmates serving multiple sentences either have consecutive, or "stacked", terms, or they are concurrent, or "running cc." If they are consecutive, an inmate must earn enough good time on the first to be eligible for parole before beginning to earn good time on the second, and so on. Credit for one is not awarded to the next. If they are concurrent, for all intents and purposes, he has one sentence, and credit for one—the longest— is awarded to all and "eats up" the shorter one.

count time. Actual headcount of all inmates on a particular unit. Taken at the same time each day, at least, and not restricted to, 7 A.M., 9 A.M., 1 P.M., 3 P.M., 7 P.M., 10 P.M., and 1 A.M. in all Texas prisons.

custody. The designation that determines the level of security an inmate must endure and the privileges he is allowed. Custody levels are technically G1, G2, G3, G4, and G5, but more familiarly are called maximum, close, medium, and minimum, with privileges rising accordingly. Also called status.

drive-ups. New inmates.

EA scores. Educational achievement scores from a test given to determine an inmate's eligibility for various prison educational programs. Maximum score is 12.9. Used only for in-prison programs, this has questionable validity and no free-world relevancy.

GP. The general population of the prison, as opposed to protective custody.

good time. Simply put, good time is time, figured in days, awarded for being "good" enough to be promoted to a certain class.

in and outs. Those times inmates can exit or enter the dayrooms from their cells.

Johnnies. The sack lunches given to inmates who otherwise are prevented from going to the chow hall to eat. Inmates on lockdown are fed nothing but Johnnies. Usually a meat sandwich, a peanut butter and jelly sandwich, some raisins, and a half-pint of milk.

lay-in. A pass ordering an inmate to report to a certain place at a certain time, for medical appointments, parole interviews, etc. Lay-ins are usually scheduled so as not to interfere with work, but if issued during work hours, they take precedence over work and excuse inmates from their jobs.

lead row. The inmate who serves as the leader of a work squad.

line. A job assignment involving mostly outdoor, agricultural labor done by twenty to forty inmates in squads. Always supervised by armed officers on horseback, the line is where most incoming, physically fit inmates are assigned, and where most medium and all close custody inmates are assigned. Only medical infirmity exempts an inmate from the line. Also called hoe squads, field squads, and work squads.

necessities. Clothing and linen exchange, both the exchange and actual item (shorts, shirts, pants, socks, sheets, and pillowcases,) as well as the department, usually connected to the laundry, which provides them.

ODR. The Officer's Dining Room, an eating area reserved for officers and staffed by inmates, who also prepare the food. Considered one of the more prestigious jobs in prison for an inmate. Free-world employees and TDCJ staff are supposed to sign for and pay for meals eaten in the ODR but do so only sporadically. Officially, the menus are the same—officers eat what inmates eat. However, if inmates are served baked chicken, officers get barbecued or fried chicken; if inmates are served gelatin, officers receive cinnamon rolls, etc. Inmates who work in the ODR usually must meet the approval of at least the building captain and are usually issued tailored, pressed clothing.

PC. Protective custody, a status accorded to inmates who have proved they will be preyed upon—physically, sexually or financially—by either staff or inmates, if left in general population. One type of PC, granted to inmates who actually fear for their life, is placement in ad/seg. Another, usually reserved for admitted homosexuals, is to place them in safe-keeping status, housing them together and allowing them to work with only each other, or with other general population inmates only under strict supervision.

PHD. Pre-hearing detention. A temporary status given to inmates who are kept in isolation while an investigation determines the particulars of a charge or an accusation.

picket. An enclosure for guards in control of hallways or inmate living quarters. Pickets contain controls for lights and doors, telephones, gas masks, gas canisters, and other riot equipment. On older units, pickets are in the hallways, at the end of the blocks. Door controls may be manual or electric, and officers must continually run up and down stairs, opening the doors by hand every half-hour or hour. On newer units, pickets are in the center of three or four pods. These pickets are glass-sided and offer unimpeded view of blocks and runs. The controls are all electronic, and officers need only push a button to open the cell doors. Sometimes, the guntowers on the outside fences are also called pickets.

piddle. To make craft goods for sale; a piddler is the inmate who makes the craft.

pill call. When prescription medications are passed out.

privilege. Something earned that can be withdrawn for rules violations. Examples: parole, visits, televisions, weights for the weight lifters. Not to be confused with rights, which are guaranteed through state or federal constitution, or by law, such as access to the courts and mail.

run. The concrete walkways providing access to cells.

sap. A makeshift weapon, usually a heavy object placed in a sock to be swung against the opponent.

SAT. State Approved Trusty.

shakedown. A search of an inmate or his living quarters. Can be random—officers are expected to shakedown a few cells each shift and to pat search the occasional inmate. In theory, the threat of its randomness should inhibit smuggling. Can be scheduled and massive, as when a unit is placed on lockdown for a few days to search for drugs or weapons, especially if officials fear rioting after a period of excessive violence. Inmates can be ordered to strip anywhere, at any time, for any reason. Thus shakedowns are a harassment technique favored by a certain type of officer, who will leave an inmate's cell a chaotic mess, with belongings of a personal nature destroyed, or who will force an inmate to strip naked in the hallway or outside in the freezing weather. The humiliation and frustration caused by repeated shake-downs will cause many inmates to retaliate and are the cause of numerous incidents of inmate-on-staff violence.

shank. A makeshift knife.

spread. Any meal fixed by inmates involving heating and mixing of canned goods they have purchased in the commissary.

SSI. Abbreviation for Support Service Inmates, of which there are two types—orderlies and clerks. Orderlies are basically janitors, who keep cellblocks, hallways, and administrative areas clean. They are allowed movement not allowed to other inmates—down hallways, on the runs, and to living areas other than their own (which makes them prized smugglers). Clerks perform filing, typing, and record-keeping duties that do not involve the handling of sensitive data. Many work on top-of-the-line computers and, due to their diligence and competence, are almost indispensable to the area which they are assigned. However, no computer that any inmate has access to has a modem, thus no inmate has access to the Internet. Both clerk and orderly Support Service Inmates must be approved by the Unit and State Classification Committees, and are automatically stripped of their jobs for at least three years upon conviction of a major disciplinary case.

status. The designation that determines the level of security an inmate must endure and the privileges he is allowed. Status levels are technically G1, G2, G3, G4, and G5, but more familiarly are called maximum, close, medium, and minimum, with privileges rising accordingly. Also called class.

store. The prison commissary, sometimes called the canteen, where inmates (and officers) are allowed to buy the foodstuffs and dry goods that a particular unit offers. Think of a walk-by convenience store, with you standing in a window and presenting your written order to the clerk.

TDC. Texas Department of Corrections.

TDCJ. Texas Department of Criminal Justice.

transient. A temporary status given to an inmate who is unassigned due to unavailability of appropriate housing, or because he is in transit from unit to unit. Also, the area designated for such inmates.

turnouts. Men who have been coerced into sex.

writ-writer. An inmate well-versed in the law and in TDCJ regulations or administrative directives, who frequents the library and files briefs or assists others in legal matters.

Index

*Note: Page numbers in **bold** refer to main topics